LOVE Aflame

Karen and Ron Flowers

REVIEW AND HERALD® PUBLISHING ASSOCIATION
HAGERSTOWN, MD 21740

Unless otherwise noted, Bible texts in this book are from The New King James Version. Copyright © 1979, 1980, 1982, Thomas Nelson, Inc., Publishers.

Texts credited to NEB are from *The New English Bible*. © The Delegates of the Oxford University Press and the Syndics of the Cambridge University Press 1961, 1970. Reprinted by permission.

Texts credited to NIV are from the *Holy Bible, New International Version*. Copyright © 1973, 1978, 1984, International Bible Society. Used by permission of Zondervan Bible Publishers.

Bible texts credited to NRSV are from the New Revised Standard Version of the Bible, copyright © 1989 by the Division of Christian Education of the National Council of the Churches of Christ in the U.S.A. Used by permission.

Bible texts credited to RSV are from the Revised Standard Version of the Bible, copyright © 1946, 1952, 1971, by the Division of Christian Education of the National Council of the Churches of Christ in the U.S.A. Used by permission.

Bible texts credited to TEV are from the *Good News Bible*—Old Testament: Copyright © American Bible Society 1976; New Testament: Copyright © American Bible Society 1966, 1971, 1976.

Verses marked TLB are taken from *The Living Bible*, copyright © 1971 by Tyndale House Publishers, Wheaton, Ill. Used by permission.

This book was
Edited by Gerald Wheeler
Designed by Bill Kirstein
Cover design by Helcio Deslandes
Typeset: 11/12 Times

PRINTED IN U.S.A.

97 96 95 94 93 92   10 9 8 7 6 5 4 3 2 1

Library of Congress Cataloging in Publication Data
Flowers, Karen, 1945-
    Love aflame / Karen and Ron Flowers.
       p.   cm.
    1. Bible. O.T. Song of Solomon—Criticism, interpretation, etc.
I. Flowers, Ron, 1944-   . II. Title.
BS1485.2.F56   1992
223'.906—dc20   92-2287
                                                CIP

ISBN 0-8280-0690-3

Contents

Introduction

Songs of love flourish in every generation because God created human beings for relationships. That Scripture preserves one such song draws the curtain back on God, illuminating Him for all time as One who smiled with great delight on His creation in the beginning and who has not changed His mind about the goodness of all that He has made.

Despite the tragic free-fall in human relationships from the perfection of the beginning to the brokenness that marks the end-time, the haunting melody of Eden still lingers. In dark times over the centuries and in the painful life experiences of many, the song of love can scarcely be picked out of the discord, but the Song of Songs represents a grand prelude to the day when, in Jesus Christ, the fully orchestrated symphony of human intimacy with God and with each other will again be heard.

Whether you seek a one-finger melody to meet the needs of your own soul, or to blend your voice in more perfect harmony with that of another, or whether you yearn for the restoration of the majestic themes of coregency and oneness that vibrated through human instruments when the world was a paradise, the Song of Songs plays for you.

> "Rise up, my love, my fair one,
> And come away.
> For lo, the winter is past,
> The rain is over and gone.
> The flowers appear on the earth;
> The time of singing . . . is come!"
> —S. of Sol. 2:10-12

CHAPTER 1

What Would Solomon Know?

"Congratulations," began the terse note we received while working on the manuscript for *Love Aflame*. "You are certainly to be commended if you can find truth about marriage in the writings of a polygamist!" Not the first to express skepticism on the qualification of King Solomon to speak on love, our friend's mixture of humor and sarcasm nonetheless caused us pause. Why were we writing a book on the Song of Songs? What would Solomon know about true love and marriage? By what ironic twist is his love song preserved for all time, even stamped with Inspiration's imprimatur?

What could Solomon say, for example, to our friends Maria and Carlos, who are coming each week for premarital guidance, poised on the brink of covenant and new levels of intimacy? What does he understand about the ebb and flow of married love, of how the moments of ecstasy vanish in the scores of humdrum days of living side by side?

What would he know about the violence that has destroyed every vestige of the young love that once brought John and Christina to the altar? Even a man whose wisdom is proverbial would be hard pressed to find words for Allissa, the victim of her father's lusts, who cannot see beyond her pain to a relationship of trust with any man.

And what of Harold and Nelma, whose marriage of nearly 50 years has made them a wellspring of wisdom of their own? Can Solomon teach them anything new? Or Cindy, or Tom, or Chris, or Kit, whose intimacy needs run deep, but who fulfill their needs not through marriage but through family and friends? If Solomon on love is worth anything, is it for marrieds only?

Or what of Solomon's relevance to Anne and Emily, Raj and Matthew, children whose bodies have yet to awaken any interests beyond dolls and tree houses and friends like themselves?

What will Solomon say to Tom and Sue, who slip silently now through different doors to different pews, desperately seeking new love, new hope, new beginnings in the wake of painful domestic tragedy? What good is love poetry, anyway, by Solomon—or anybody else?

Now that's more than a bookful of questions, and we may yet regret posing some of them! But we agreed to write this book out of our experience with Scripture as a book that touches life where we live it, a book that is no stranger to brokenness, and a book that elevates pristine ideals only in the context of grace, practical help, and encouragement. So we will see what Solomon and the Song of Songs have to offer.

A Polygamist on True Love

Scripture records that Solomon had 700 wives and 300 concubines—women legally married to him, though of lesser status than his full wives (1 Kings 11:3). Many Bible students refuse to believe that he could write about love, faithfulness, and intimacy with one wife.

However, both the title to the book and tradition point to Solomon as the author. Despite the transgressions for which he became infamous, there are good reasons to believe that not only was he the author of this biblical love poem, but he composed it about the real relationship between himself and the most loved woman in his life. Furthermore, as we will see, he may well have been the best choice of all the writers upon whom God's Spirit could have called to paint this enduring word portrait of marital intimacy. For as he writes, many painful experiences focus his memory and give light and form to the beauty of what was and what might have been.

Childhood's Imprint

The roots of a marriage sink deep into the emotional soil of childhood. The circumstances surrounding the marriage of his parents, David and Bathsheba, represent the moral low point in the saga of David's life and reign. In his father's house, Solomon witnessed the ravages of adultery, murder, revenge, manipulation, anger, sibling rivalry, and hatred. All the trouble and turbulence of David's numerous marriages were open to his view, and all made their mark upon the young man.

But thankfully, his home also knew the triumph of God's grace. Despite the painful manner in which his parents began their relationship (see 2 Sam. 11), Solomon saw their love eventually develop into commitment, as evidenced by David's determination to make Bathsheba's son the heir to his throne (1 Kings 1:30). David's regard for Solomon and indications of Bathsheba's close ties with him are scattered through the narrative, giving us a glimpse into their loving care. The prophet Nathan even brings word of God's special affection for him, and ever after, he bore the nickname Jedidiah, ''beloved of Jehovah'' (see 2 Sam. 12:25).

As a youth, Solomon must have heard his father sing and pray, repenting in vivid detail of his great sin, and embracing God's immeasurable forgiveness (Ps. 51 and 32). He must have marveled at David's tangible expressions of devotion to God in the lavish preparation for the Temple construction. And so Solomon emerges, even from the midst of domestic turmoil, with a reverence for God and a sensitive heart.

Gifted by God

Solomon was a gifted writer and composed more than 1,000 songs. His abilities as an all-around naturalist drew acclaim from his own people and surrounding nations (1 Kings 4:30-34). Such familiarity with plants and animals pervades the Song of Solomon, flooding it with sights and sounds and scents that help enhance its romantic theme. The book mentions numerous perfumes and spices, along with various creatures of forest and field.

But these things were not his most important gifts. Upon his accession to the throne, God touched him in a remarkable way. His biographer devotes 11 verses to describing what happened, that posterity might never forget that the special ability he had came from God and was to be used for God. The Lord bestowed upon him "a wise and understanding heart" (1 Kings 3:12). The divine gift, referred to later as a "largeness of heart like the sand on the seashore" (1 Kings 4:29), signifies a great capacity for understanding human emotions and the principles of human relationships. This God-given endowment would open his mind to human nature and provide him with unusual insight into the laws of the mind.

Besides his psychological understanding, Solomon was himself a man of great emotional capacity. Yielded to God, his spirit was humble, sensitive, affectionate, loving, and compassionate. He was open, honest, and vulnerable, qualities that are essential to close, positive relationships. By endowing him with such capacities, God prepared him to compose the Song as well as those proverbs, psalms, and other writings attributed to him.

God intended that Solomon's "largeness of heart" should make him a wise, selfless, and compassionate leader—the Lord's undershepherd (cf. 1 Peter 5:2-4). In this sense he was a forerunner of Christ who knew the hearts and minds of people, who manifested compassion, and who showed unsurpassed insight into their needs. Turned inwardly to serve self, however, Solomon's great strength became an insatiable thirst for fame, a passion for luxury and pleasure, and a lust for the cravings and appetites of fallen human nature.

It often happens that people are most vulnerable where they appear to be the strongest. Fine traits of character are like the grain in a beautiful piece of wood. While such markings create its attractiveness, they also highlight the wood's most vulnerable points. Strike along the grain, and the wood will split, destroying its beauty and usefulness. So it was in Solomon's experience. When he took his strengths for granted, assuming them to be of his own making and thus leaving them unguarded, then he was most susceptible to Satan's attacks. And that which God gave for a blessing became a curse.

Love of His Life

By Solomon's time, marriage practices had departed far from the Edenic plan. The law of Moses discouraged polygamy, but did not prohibit it (Deut. 17:17). King David had many wives and concubines, though only the names of nine survive (2 Sam. 3; 5; 11; 1 Kings 1:3ff.). According to the custom, all these women automatically became Solomon's responsibility upon his succession to the throne. They were numbered as his, irrespective of his personal relationship with them. It is not inconceivable that the 60 queens and 80 concubines mentioned in Song of Solomon 6:8 were the harem bequeathed by his father. The casual reference Solomon makes to them does not accord them the place in his life given to Shulamith, as we will refer to his wife in the Song of Songs. She was the true love of his life. "My dove, my perfect one, is the only one" (S. of Sol. 6:9).

Though Solomon's affections eventually included the many different women he brought to Jerusalem as part of his political alliances with foreign governments (1 Kings 3:1; 11:1), the spiritual deterioration of his later years had not yet begun during the period described in the Song, for his bride indicates that good people are proud of his name (S. of Sol. 1:3) and describes his physique as strong and youthful (S. of Sol. 5:10-16). The love, affection, and intimacy recorded between them has all the earmarks of an early love, if not the first and only true love bond Solomon ever knew.

On the basis of the similarity between "Shulamite" (S. of Sol. 6:13) and "Shunammite" (1 Kings 1:3), some have speculated that the woman was Abishag, the personal attendant to David during his last days. However, the Song indicates that Solomon had personally courted the woman, and, given the references to Lebanon and its mountains (S. of Sol. 2:8; 4:8ff.), that she came from much farther north than Abishag's Shunem, located near Megiddo in the tribal territory of Issachar (Joshua 19:18). Solomon especially enjoyed Lebanon. He imported its timber for the Temple before his fourth year (1 Kings 5:14; 6:1) and apparently purchased property and built buildings there, perhaps a vacation residence (1 Kings 9:19). Scripture indicates that he had continual contact with the country at least until the thirteenth year of his reign (1 Kings 7:1). The best guess is that he found the woman described in the book during one of his trips there (cf. S. of Sol. 2:8ff.).

The love of this woman referred to as "Shulamite" (S. of Sol. 6:1), or "Shulamith," gave Solomon the experience that ultimately qualified him to write the book. In fact, though she probably never put pen to papyrus, this special piece of sacred poetry is really as much hers as his, for without the love and intimacy they knew together, the Song could never have come to be.

Their closeness did not result easily—intimacy in relationships never does. Each brought some common interests to their marriage, to be sure—a similar religious heritage, a love of the outdoors and all things created, a strong attraction for each other that led to both deep joy and profound satisfaction in each other's presence.

They each brought their pasts—both had known brokenness, shattered dreams, distress, and pain. The models they had for homelife and marriage fell short of ideal. While Scripture paints Solomon's family tree in bold relief for all to see, we can only pencil Shulamith's heritage in sketchy outline from the tiny windows into her past opened in the Song. The evidence indicates that she grew up in less than idyllic circumstances. Eking out an existence was hard, and her brothers forced her to work like a man in the vineyards. Exposure to the sun and wind left her complexion dark and swarthy, and she entered womanhood fully aware that as society around her defines beauty, she fell short of the mark.

But they were also very different in many ways. He came from the city—the royal court with its international culture, especially that of Egypt—while she brought a rural background. Solomon had traveled widely, but her experience extended only to the village near her country home. While he was familiar and at ease with the ceremonies and etiquette of the royal court, she must have felt awkward there, unsure of what would be expected of her. As the king's son he knew the luxuries of life. She had lived a harsher reality.

So their love brings them together, each bearing baggage containing the pieces of their pasts that make them who they are—some pieces broken, others whole, to be mingled together in their journey toward oneness in the relationship called marriage.

A Return to Eden

That God should inspire Solomon to leave such an intimate glimpse of their relationship for us is cause for thanksgiving and celebration. If a substantial part of the role of Scripture is to serve as a textbook on how God intends us to conduct our human relationships, then the Song of Solomon is surely a key portion of the unit on love in general and marriage in particular. In timeless fashion it addresses the fundamental human drive or hunger for intimacy and reveals much about how to meet this need, both in friendship and within the covenant of marriage.

More than one commentator has noted the similarities between Eden and the setting of the Song. "In the Song of Songs we have come full circle, in the OT, back to the Garden of Eden." [1] Nevertheless, while the Song reminds one of Eden, it's setting is not the original paradise. The couple are not the first man and woman, nor is their world a sinless one. The Song is sung against a backdrop of anger and injustice (S. of Sol. 1:6), violence and pain (S. of Sol. 5:7), even death (S. of Sol. 8:6). What we do observe in the Song is an elevation of marriage toward the ideals of Eden, a desire for its redemption to the fullest extent possible, given the setting of a fallen world in which human beings must live. "In the 'symphony of love,' begun in Eden but gone awry after the Fall, Canticles constitutes 'love's lyrics redeemed.' " [2]

Without mentioning His name, the Song affirms God's handiwork: trees, flowers, sun, moon, birds, animals. It includes human love and sexuality along with them as good gifts from the Creator's hand. The book presents the lovers as equals in every way. The word translated "Shulamite" (S. of Sol. 6:1) is in fact the feminine form of the name "Solomon." In the poem she is his opposite, his counterpart, his mirror image. The fact that, though written by Solomon, so much of the Song reflects her inner feelings reveals the openness and depth of their communication. The poem does not hide the anger and conflict that arise in all close relationships, yet it points to ways that we can bridge differences and develop deep levels of trust and confidence. Marriage in the Song is an uplifting experience of mutual caring, joy, and fulfillment.

What Might Have Been

It was God who bountifully prepared Solomon for his lifework, endowed him with profound insights into relationships, provided for him Shulamith, and gave them both the experience of love recorded in the Song. One cannot help believing that God had cast him for a far more significant role in instructing his own nation and the world about human relationships and marriage than ever played out in the drama of his life. It is sad that one so talented wandered off life's stage without saying more of his lines. A poem by John Greenleaf Whittier immediately comes to mind:

> Of all sad words of tongue or pen,
> The saddest are these: "It might have been!"

While many seek the buried treasure of marital bliss, few have uncovered as many of its precious jewels as did Solomon in his relationship with Shulamith. As grateful as we are for the Song he left us, we still feel disappointed that so little was done for marriage by one who could have done so much! He who could have elevated marriage from the depths to which it had fallen, and helped to reclaim the purity and beauty it had when it came from Paradise, rather became responsible for its further degradation.

In *Splendor of the Song of Solomon*, George T. Dickinson suggests that the book "reveals a remarkable girl who probably took hold of Solomon and dragged him away for a time at least from a threatening pit of debauchery." [3] Like many spouses who have tearfully watched their mates turn from their covenants and make ruinous choices, she must have wondered what she might have done to keep him true. However, Solomon's personal pride and ambition led him into political and commercial alliances with many nations that he sealed by marrying their princesses. He justified such marriages in his own mind with the rationale that it was a means of bringing to such nations a knowledge of the true God. And so, scarcely aware of where it would take him, Solomon blundered down the path of apostasy. Scripture details the completeness of his personal ruination. He "clung" to his heathen wives "in love" (1 Kings 11:2). They "turned his heart after other gods" and he "did evil in the sight of the Lord" (verses 4, 6).

But God in His long-suffering and compassion continued to appeal to Solomon. In later years, though with mind and body enfeebled by his degenerate life, he returned to God. Like Samson of old, who also squandered his spiritual gifts but then repented and used his strength at the end to salvage something of what had been lost, Solomon sought to impart the insights gained over his lifetime to light the way for those who walked the path behind him. In the writings of his old age we see our gracious God working good even out of tragedy.

Though we do not know for sure when Solomon wrote the Song, elements in it mirror the sentiments and wisdom of his later writings. There, in reflection, he sought to unfold for youth secrets of a love so intimate it must be protected by the marriage covenant. He encouraged them to guard their purity by watchfulness and prayer. Repeatedly he counsels, "Do not arouse or awaken love until it so desires" (S. of Sol. 2:7; 3:5; 8:4, NIV).

We Need the Wisdom of Solomon

What would Solomon know, then? More than we at first give him credit for. Our all-too-human author was a man of passions like us, a sinner saved by grace. We should never discredit his writings because of his sins and failings.

Scripture from Genesis to Revelation weaves the story of men and women, not in dazzling golden threads that blind us to their faults and foibles, but rather in common homespun, telling their stories simply and openly for all to see. The writers keep no secrets about their struggles and failings, else we would be left in despair because of the perfection that we would think we see in their lives. But neither can they be restrained when they themselves or others whose experiences they chronicle are touched by grace, that we might have hope.

Could we hear Solomon's voice today, we feel sure he would again be singing. Despite regrets about what might have been, his song of love beckons us beyond mistakes and failures and mundane existence to a new vision of what it means to live together, to love each other, in Christ. In Him we can no longer be content with fragmented melodies. A new song awaits to be sung, and He bids us join the chorus!

---

[1] Richard M. Davidson, "Theology of Sexuality in the Song of Songs: Return to Eden," *Andrews University Seminary Studies* 27 (No. 1): 5.

[2] Phyllis Trible, *God and the Rhetoric of Sexuality* (Philadelphia: Fortress Press, 1978), p. 144.

[3] George T. Dickinson, *Splendor of the Song of Solomon* (Washington, D.C.: Review and Herald Pub. Assn., 1971), pp. 7, 8.

CHAPTER 2

Wanted: Singers for a Love Song

For two weeks running, the following quarter-page ad appeared in our church bulletin:

CHOIR POSITIONS AVAILABLE

Positions open for:	Sopranos, altos, tenors, basses
Qualifications:	Must be able to carry light music folder up two steps into choir loft
Expertise:	Will take anyone who has sung, yodeled, hummed, or whistled in bathtub/shower
Benefits:	Quarterly fellowship potluck with other members
Hours:	Negotiable

Equal opportunity employer.
Please apply in time for practice Friday night at 7:30!

Our congregation has some wonderful singers, but not enough to make a choir. I guess that's why the choir director ran the ad. Anyway, quite a few responded. Never mind that one or two can sing only the melody no matter what part carries it, and the director's own husband has been known to ask what that note with the funny little flag on it means. They'll sound great by Christmas!

We Can Have Better Relationships

So what does all this have to do with Solomon's Song? In one encouraging sentence: God can make a singer out of anyone! Though forming and maintaining good relationships comes easier for some than others, success as a brother, sister, husband, wife, parent, or friend is not reserved only for "naturals" or those lucky enough to watch good role models at close hand. The great news is that we can *learn* to have better relationships. Relational skills are not magical endowments bestowed only on a chosen few. We can all discover how to read the music and join the chorus.

We count our personal acquaintance with the late David Mace and his wife, Vera, one of life's highest privileges. David and Vera together founded the Association of Couples for Marriage Enrichment, an international organization whose ministry has strengthened thousands of marriages worldwide.

At our first marriage enrichment training event with David and Vera, heavy fog settled low over the North Carolina mountain retreat center, pulling the shades on the outside world down around 12 couples gathered to sit at the feet of the famous elderly pair. Pitched together during the war years in a ministry for Christian young people in Britain, the two had established respect for each other long before love blossomed. But even then they had found each other difficult. David was the epitome of structure and organization, while Vera approached life from a less regimented perspective. Even now, more than a decade into retirement and past their fiftieth wedding anniversary, she still muttered with a half smile of resignation that his bent toward timing all our activities to the second paralyzed her brain!

How we wish we could create on paper our experience of entering into their lives as a couple through their dialogues that weekend. Theirs had not been an easy marriage. Differences that at first attracted had become like burrs that created festering wounds under constant pressure and friction. Stubbornness and anger had reared up between them, forcing two who would be one flesh further apart, it seemed, than when they had started. But determined to find the pathway to intimacy together, they had forged out the principles of love for their own relationship. And now they were translating them for generations of would-be-lovers to follow. Etched indelibly on our minds is the vision of this thin, balding husband leaning close and shouting tenderly into the face of his snowy-haired, nearly deaf beloved, both earnestly struggling to understand each other and to grow together in love literally until death did them part.

We take courage from the Davids and Veras in our experience. If loving can be learned, then we are eager to be about it. Having known the igniting spark, we now seek the fuel to sustain love's flame over a lifetime. And we believe it is to be found in Scripture.

Scripture: A Textbook on Relationships

You may need some new glasses to see Scripture as a book about relationships. Usually we don theological spectacles for Bible study. But in this book we will look at Scripture through family glasses. Their tint will not restrict our theological vision, but it will cast a relational hue over familiar passages that we may not have focused on as carefully from such a perspective.

The Bible's instruction about relationships comes packaged in several wrappings, some well-defined and precise in their patterns, others whose designs have more subtle hues and forms. But each provides a significant piece of the mosaic of God's original plan.

Relational directives. In bold, distinct lines the Bible offers a basic framework for getting along with each other. It contains directives for married couples, parents, children, neighbors, friends. For example, they include:

> Drink water from your own cistern,
> And running water from your own well. . . .
> Rejoice with the wife of your youth . . .
> And always be enraptured with her love (Prov. 5:15-19).

> Children, obey your parents in all things, for this is well pleasing to the Lord. Fathers, do not provoke your children, lest they become discouraged (Col. 3:20, 21).

> Do not devise evil against your neighbor,
> For he dwells by you for safety's sake (Prov. 3:29).

To him who is afflicted, kindness should be shown by his friend (Job 6:14).

Overarching general principles spread an umbrella over all the relationship instruction in the Bible, such as the golden rule (Matt. 7:12) and Christ's summing up of the law into the two great commandments (Matt. 22:36-40). They are lofty ideals to stretch toward:

> Love your enemies, do good to those who hate you, bless those who curse you, and pray for those who spitefully use you. To him who strikes you on the one cheek, offer the other also. And from him who takes away your cloak, do not withhold your tunic either (Luke 6:27-29).

> If it is possible, as much as depends on you, live peaceably with all men (Rom. 12:18).

> Let nothing be done through selfish ambition or conceit, but in lowliness of mind let each esteem others better than himself (Phil. 2:3).

Yet while the gospel continually calls us to the highest pinnacles of Christian living in our relationships with others, God never makes our climb toward the summit our ticket to heaven. Our salvation is in Christ alone, who came to redeem and restore all that sin has broken. Biblical ideals shine forth as stars by which to steer our course, yet they are set against a backdrop of grace. Scripture recognizes the imperfections of our attitudes and behaviors (Rom. 7:19; Gal. 5:17) even as we live our lives as Christians. We shall need to forgive and be forgiven in our relationships (Eph. 4:31, 32). And we shall have frequent occasion to confess our faults one to another and pray for each other (James 5:16). Led by the Spirit, we grow in love.

Stories for all ages. One of God's most stunning gift wraps for relational truth is something so simple in its design that we often pass over it as of little consequence. Stories are for kids, we say, and with that we relegate the narratives of Scripture to children's books and games of Bible trivia. Family glasses, however, cause us to stop for another look. Take, for instance, one old familiar story . . .

Her eyes squinted in the haze. Rising up out of the parched landscape in the distance, the walls of an ancient city hugged the people and places and things she had once called home.

She didn't wish for memories, but they came anyway. Famine aside, life had been so full of promise when they left. Her husband was strong and in the prime of life. She was secure in his love, and together they were looking out for the best for their family. God had smiled on them, then, making their necessary sojourn into a foreign land more of an adventure than a trial. Funny, she couldn't even picture God with a smile now. First the shock of her husband's unexpected death had made her world go black. But she had fought her way back, coped with the grief, the loneliness, the fear, the overload. She had raised two boys by herself and seen them establish homes of their own. In them had rested her hope, her future. Her dreams would live out in their lives. But a cruel fate had snatched them, too. And now her darkness was so intense that even the sights and sounds of home brought not the slightest glimmer of hope.

A light footstep beside her jolted her into an awareness that she was not alone in her misery. Out of custom her two daughters-in-law had come with her, both now single again as well. She had carefully rehearsed her speech, not wanting to be insensitive or ungrateful. After all, she did love them. One had turned and waved goodbye. But this one had dogged her footsteps mile after weary mile across the desolate rift valley and up into the Judean hills.

How futile the girl's words seemed. "Your people shall be my people." What people? Didn't she know her mother-in-law's womb was forever barren, her heirs dead? And "your God, my God" (Ruth 1:16). What a God He had turned out to be!

She did not speak, but out of the corner of her eye glanced at the younger woman beside her. Now there would be two mouths to feed, more of the dismal story that would have to be told. Yet something about her made it hard to resent her quiet presence.

So Naomi bade her follow, as with a worn sleeve she mopped the sweat from her forehead and adjusted the heavy sack that held all the remnants of her past and her only stake in the future.

Thus did Naomi and Ruth return to Bethlehem "at the beginning of barley harvest" (Ruth 1:22).

The Bible is often terse in its storytelling and significant in both the details it reveals and those it omits. Sometimes one has to read a bit between the lines to put flesh on all the characters and bring the setting up in vivid color.

Of course, there is much more to this story. What we have detailed is but the first of several scenes that portray relational issues. Rodgers and Hammerstein could have made a classic out of the story. How *do* you solve a problem like Naomi's?

Her story not only opens a psychological window on the human quest for personal worth and the predictable process of dealing with grief and loss, but also raises basic questions about sin and suffering and who God is and what His role is in all of it. The book of Ruth offers temperament and personality portraits to study and human development continuums to observe. We see stages of faith to contrast, and marriage and parenting patterns that reflect both unique cultural settings and biblical principles that apply for all time. Real people face real life in real families, finding real healing in a vibrant, loving community that cares for their own as well as the strangers that darken their doors. A lover's redemptive act gestures through the centuries to One who loves with an everlasting love, One who will never let us go. And a child softens the painful memories and provides hope and joy for the future.

From Genesis to Revelation the Bible abounds with stories that present a rich diadem of relational truth. As we lift them to the light, lessons glint and glisten from every jewel to enrich our lives in our families, among our friends, and as witnesses for Christ in the communities where we live.

Relational laws and probabilities. One of life's great joys is finding a kindred spirit. From my own personal experience I know that the delight of such discoveries intensifies just from their very rarity. And surely one of my most treasured finds is my friend Nelm. Twenty years separate our ages, so our oneness of soul runs much deeper than generational kinship. But somehow it doesn't seem right to analyze and probe the whys and wherefores of such a friendship anyway. I simply love this woman, and I know she loves me.

One of the things I love about Nelm is her pithy wisdom. Once when we were knitting together, I noticed that she had made a rather obvious mistake many rows back in a fairly complicated sweater pattern. Thinking she would be discouraged when she saw it, I mentally decided to take it out that night and catch her up to where she had been by morning. But when she held her work up for admiration and found the mistake herself, it caused her only a moment's dismay. "Oh well," she giggled, "it's the perfect place to sew a butterfly! Anyway," she went on, "as my grandmother would have said, 'It will never be seen from a galloping horse!' " And I knew again why I like her. She's always willing to sew a butterfly over my flaws and will never hastily abandon our friendship. Nelm's just full of this kind of *Poor Richard's Almanac* filler, and, as I think about it, she could give Ben Franklin a run for his money in the area of both insights into human nature and common sense!

The Bible, too, packages much of its wisdom about relationships in pithy, common sense statements about human nature and observable relational law and probability. For starters:

A soft answer turns away wrath,
But a harsh word stirs up anger (Prov. 15:1).

Anxiety in the heart of a man causes depression,
But a good word makes it glad (Prov. 12:25).

A whisperer separates the best of friends (Prov. 16:28).

Open rebuke is better than love carefully concealed (Prov. 27:5).

Train up a child in the way he should go, and when he is old he will not depart from it (Prov. 22:6).

A man who has friends must himself be friendly (Prov. 18:24).

While experience causes us to nod our heads in confirmation of the truths embodied in such proverbs, the insights they offer into human nature and the inner workings of relationships are nonetheless profound. And once again Scripture affirms our basic human need for meaningful relationships and our responsibility to one another as a human family, and leads us by its wisdom to new and deeper levels of understanding and covenant in Christ.

The Role of the Song of Songs
The Song of Songs stands alone in Scripture as the longest

piece dedicated solely to a relational theme. But the nature of the
poem defies its easy grouping with other kinds of biblical thought
on relational living. While it has narrative elements, the frag-
ments are so sketchy that the poem resists definition simply as a
love story. Perhaps Solomon intended it that way, since, as we
shall see in the next chapter, the Song does not so much relate a
narrative as disclose the essence of human intimacy.

Some may be tempted to minimize the Song as relational
instruction since on the surface it parades no relational directives,
no pithy wisdom sayings, no quickly discernible relational law.
But we must not be hasty. The Song's wisdom runs deep. Its
lessons are subtle, and the reader often responds to them through
his emotions before he can even verbalize them. In ways and to
depths not possible through other mediums, the Song unfolds the
anatomy of human intimacy and offers Scripture's best insights
into how we form and maintain relationships.

Spiritual Significance in Human Relationships

Why so much emphasis on human relationships in Scripture?
Isn't the Bible primarily concerned about God and His dealings
with human individuals and our personal response to Him?

When I was a girl growing up, a certain man in our
community had a widespread reputation for his piety and sacrifice. He was a thin little man who kept dried seaweed in his
pockets instead of jelly beans. But when the church refinished the
basement, he gave a lot of money and worked scores of
dawn-to-dusk Sundays until it was finished. Mr. Jones personally
paid for and serviced the literature rack in the town laundromat.
And when an evangelist set up his tent during off-season on the
carnival grounds, he passed out more handbills than anyone.
Always present at prayer meeting, he was the only adult I knew
who could say all his memory verses. I remember thinking he'd
surely go to heaven because he was so good.

It's only now that I'm older and have learned a few things that
some of the memories of the man and his family now haunt me.
You never saw much of Mrs. Jones. She was always busy with
the kids, and they were sick much of the time. Their house
needed a lot of repair, though she kept things up as best she

could. My mom gave her a flat of pansies once in the spring, and tears came to her eyes. I can't remember ever seeing her in a new dress.

The incongruities of all this largely passed me by in child-hood, but Scripture opens to the discerning eye the understanding that in such not-so-uncommon situations, something is awry.

Scripture addresses human beings as a package, because that's the way God created us. While we may label the individual facets of the human crystal separately as physical, intellectual, emotional, spiritual, and social components, only together can they function as fully human. Despite the earnest and sincere attempts of "saints" down through the ages to develop their spiritual—and perhaps intellectual—dimensions to the neglect, even denial, of their physical, social, and emotional selves, the human being resists segmentation. We cannot break ourselves into separate and isolated categories. Therefore, we should not be surprised that the Bible addresses us in wholistic terms. It begins with the assumption that God created every aspect of our human nature in the beginning and declared them to be very good. And it builds on the premise that, though perverted by sin, everything that God made and called very good He can make new in Jesus Christ.

I have no doubt in my mind that Mr. Jones wanted to be a Christian. But if one can judge from the sidelines—which I admit is a very dangerous thing to do—it appears as if, in his quest for things spiritual, he may have missed a vital linkage with things relational.

But even as I write, I'm not really thinking about Mr. Jones. I can't even remember his real name. I'm thinking about Ron and Karen and Jeff and Jon—a family struggling to find balance in their lives, to set the right priorities, to discover how Bible truth plays out in the real life of Christians who need redemption for every aspect of their humanness.

Jesus left no doubt that, as regards the law, our behavior in human relationships holds equal status with our conduct in relation to God. In fact, any attempt to separate the two is artificial. He said that there exist only two great commandments. They defined the parameters of the two tablets of the law at Sinai, and He reiterated them as He talked law with the Pharisees: " 'You shall love the Lord your God with all your heart, with all your soul, and with all your mind.'. . . And . . .'You shall love your neighbor as yourself.' On these two commandments hang all the Law and the Prophets" (Matt. 22:37-40). Paul reduced the entire law to loving one's neighbor (Gal. 5:14), understanding instinctively that it was the harder side of the equation, the surest evidence of true love for God.

Jesus gave spiritual significance to relationships for three vital reasons. First, human beings need human love to comprehend God's love. God refers to Himself as father, mother, and husband (Ps. 103:13; Is. 66:13; 54:5), imagery speaking of nurture, comfort, security, and love. But such imagery loses its meaning and—even worse—becomes perverted and destroyed for those whose families have shrouded their entire lives in pain and darkness.

We knew a man once who had been a leader in his church for many years. When we came to that congregation, he held office as elder, treasurer, personal ministries leader, and Sabbath school teacher. Not long after my arrival as pastor, an elderly widow in the church took me aside and, with conflicting emotions because of her great respect for the elder, spilled out the details of things happening at church on the weeks I could not be there. While the man, who had brought a number of the members into the church, was sincere in his preaching and teaching, the congregation was becoming more and more discouraged. Whether in tithe or offerings, in Bible study or missionary activities, it seemed as if they could never be good enough to please him.

Since hers was not the only such report, I knew I must talk to him. With a trepidation familiar to pastors whose local elders have more experience than they do, I phoned to set an appointment with him. The brief conversation itself brought such pain in my stomach that I could neither sit nor stand nor lie down all night. I thought at first that Karen had fed me bad peanut butter.

When I arrived the next day, we briefly talked of trivia, then I began to share my concerns. I was not prepared for his response. The stately old gentleman suddenly clutched his head in his hands and began to weep, great convulsive sobs that came from deep within. When he could at last speak, he told me the story of a little boy—a little boy who wanted more than anything to please his father, but could not. No matter what he did, it was never good enough, and he received emotional and physical abuse. "I can't understand God as a loving father," he confided with a fresh burst of tears. "I have never known a father's love." His painful account of his personal childhood explained a lot of things.

God has filled Scripture with help for relationships because He knows many will never dare to believe God loves them until they feel the warmth of human affection. Every day in our families, we either tear down or build up one another's relationship with Jesus. That alone is reason enough to plumb the depths of God's instruction about relationships.

But God also elevates relational issues to a spiritual plane for a second reason. It is through love for each other that we manifest love for God. Jesus painted a picture of the end-time when saints will be surprised to find themselves counted among the righteous, and when they ask why, He will respond, "Inasmuch as you did it [showed love] to one of the least of these My brethren, you did it to Me" (Matt. 25:40). The surest proof of our acceptance of Christ's atoning righteousness will be how we have let Him make us loving and lovable Christians.

A letter arrived while we were writing this chapter. It came from a church elder looking for someone to talk to about a very difficult, potentially divisive situation through which he is trying to shepherd his congregation. "Sometimes," he wrote, "I just don't know how to bring them together." While there are no simple answers to situations as complex as he faces, sometimes we wonder how things might change if we understood that our highest worship reaches heaven when we treat each other with love.

But there remains one more reason that Scripture is awash with relational teaching, and that our success at relationships carries such spiritual weight. And that is simply "that the world may know." Jesus said, "Love one another, as I have loved you" for "by this all will know that you are My disciples" (John 13:34, 35).

Great teachers have come and gone for centuries, but none have changed history like Jesus of Nazareth. Millions still await word of Him. Countless thousands look on with a question for those of us who claim to be His followers: "Who do you say that He is?" The way we maintain relationships with each other constitutes the most significant part of our response. They may never hear our answer to their question until they stand in awe of our love.

CHAPTER 3

The Language of Love

Poetry and music have always been the language of love. Though every era has had its own style and form and expectations, the Song of Songs has stood the test of time to take its place among the best.

Solomon's philosophy of poetry would probably have found kindred spirits among the nineteenth-century English Romantic poets. In the early 1800s William Wordsworth offered to the world a new volume of poems with a fascinating preface.[1] His poems, he explained, were different from what his readers might be accustomed to, so he had written a brief introduction to them. Poetry, he affirmed, is for common people, not just an elite few given to the arts. Poets are real people who live life where the rest of us live it. Their gift lies in their capacity for feeling, their insights into human nature, their love of life, and their ability to express thoughts and emotions common to us all.

Though Solomon and the Song of Songs were no doubt far from Wordsworth's mind as he penned his preface, he could not have offered a more accurate description of this ancient piece of sacred Hebrew literature nor of the intent of its writer. Of the 1,005 songs Solomon reportedly composed (1 Kings 4:32), the Song of Solomon is acclaimed as superior among them (S. of Sol. 1:1). Crafted in the simple rustic style of Eastern idyll poetry, the Song portrays with the most delicate terms, with the most vivid poetic imagery, the attraction, the passion, the tenderness, and the unbounded delights of intimacy between the king with the wise and understanding heart and his most beloved queen. Even the casual reader cannot help being carried aloft on the heights of the poetic eloquence displayed within this crown jewel of all Hebrew poetry. For its profound insights into human nature, its forthright expression of feelings known to us all, for the manner in which it hallows "the way of a man with a maid" (Prov. 30:19, KJV), it is without peer in Scripture.

A Unique Dialogue Style

Commentators have observed that the Song of Solomon is the only book in the Bible that employs a dialogue style from beginning to end. The author placed all its content in the mouths of speakers. Some have thought of it as a drama intended to be acted or sung on stage. The dramatic theory of interpretation, though, demands considerable adjustment to the text and the imagination of a storyline. We shall see later that the poem has its own special design to fit its intended purpose.

The original Hebrew text does not designate the speakers, but by observing the shifts in gender in the words used, scholars have been able to distinguish two principal speakers, a female and a male, with several other lesser speakers. Modern Bible versions commonly divide the script of the Song of Solomon into the various parts according to the major and minor speakers.

The female speaker appears most frequently in the Song. Only once does she receive any kind of formal name or title (S. of Sol. 6:13), and this is usually translated "Shulamite" or "maid of Shulam" (TLB), as if to designate her native village. In Hebrew, however, the word is the feminine form of the name "Solomon," implying not her hometown, but her relationship to Solomon as his counterpart. Perhaps we could render the term as a title, such as "Lady Solomon." We like the more personal name "Shulamith" coined by Franz Delitzsch in his commentary *The Song of Songs and Ecclesiastes*. The male speaker (Solomon) affectionately calls her *rayahti*, "my love," literally meaning "dearest friend of mine" (S. of Sol. 1:9, 15; 4:1, 7, etc.).

Elsewhere he refers to her as "my bride," "my spouse," "my dove," "my perfect one," and also "my sister" (S. of Sol. 4:9, 10, 12; 5:1; 6:9), a term of endearment for a lover appearing in other ancient Near Eastern poetry.

The male speaker is the author himself, Solomon. Shulamith refers to him by name (S. of Sol. 3:11; 8:11, 12). She also calls him "the king" (S. of Sol. 1:4, 12), "the one I love" (literally, "he whom my soul loves" [S. of Sol. 3:1-4]), but more generally uses *dodi* "my beloved," literally "my lover" (S. of Sol. 2:8, 10, 16, 17, etc.).

Other characters in the Song include the "daughters of Jerusalem" ("women of Jerusalem" [TEV]; "young women of Jerusalem" [TLB]) who are both spoken to (S. of Sol. 1:5; 2:7; 3:5, etc.) and speak themselves (S. of Sol. 1:4; 5:9, etc.). They may have been the personal attendants of the queen, similar to the seven maidservants of Esther in the palace of Ahasuerus (Esther 2:9). Although the dialogues with them may have had some basis in real life episodes, in the Song they are not intended to be taken as actual conversations, but rather as a poetic device to develop the ideas in the poem, to mark transitions, and to emphasize certain points. Shulamith's brothers and friends of the couple also speak. While final identification of the speakers in some instances is difficult, the dialogue in the Song may be assigned as shown in Appendix A, p. 135.

At times the dialogue employs third person pronouns rather than second person. The first line of the poem is a good example: "Let *him* kiss me with the kisses of *his* mouth—for *your* love is better than wine" (S. of Sol. 1:2). Such shifts are common in Hebrew poetry. The Revised Standard Version captures the meaning: "O that you would kiss me with the kisses of your mouth! For your love is better than wine." Other examples of such shifts appear elsewhere in the Hebrew Scriptures: Psalm 23—"The Lord is my shepherd . . . *He* makes me . . . *You* are with me; *Your* rod and *Your* staff . . ." (See also Deut. 32:15; Isa. 1:29; Jer. 22:24; Micah 7:19; Amos 4:1.)

The Elusive Story

In terms of historical details, the facts of the story are

virtually impossible to assemble from the poem itself, and Solomon's biographers provide no help. The books of Kings and Chronicles record his marriage to Pharaoh's daughter, but the point of interest there for the writer is the radical shift in foreign policy toward Egypt, Israel's former enemy (1 Kings 3:1). Scripture mentions other wives (1 Kings 11:1; 14:21), including Naamah, the mother of Solomon's son and successor Rehoboam, but the historical sources identify none of them as the love of his life with whom he shared the experiences in the Song.

The difficulties involved in piecing together the story line, of seeing in Solomon a good example of a husband, or of finding a rationale for the explicit sexual imagery of the Song have led to a vast variety of interpretations. In fact, the prevailing view for centuries has been that the poem is not really about Solomon and one of his wives at all, but is really an allegory or typology of the love of God for His people (see chapter 4). Some scholars think the material originated in pagan fertility rites. Others, as we previously mentioned, see it as a dramatic script written to be acted and sung on stage, while still others regard it as nothing more than a disjointed patchwork of love lyrics Solomon brought together perhaps after the fashion of his Proverbs collection. Those who hold a natural or literal interpretation accept the Song for what it appears naturally to be—a poem that speaks clearly and explicitly of the feelings, desires, hopes, and fears of Solomon and a country girl without any need to allegorize, typologize, or dramatize the more sensual elements of the text.

Recently some have adopted a view that casts Solomon as an antagonist, with the lovers being Shulamith and an unnamed shepherd. According to this theory Shulamith resisted the king's advances and, despite being taken to the palace, remained true to her shepherd lover. Eventually the king, failing to win her affections, allowed her to return to her true love. Such an interpretation apparently arose because of references to shepherding (S. of Sol. 1:7, 8), a work that Solomon never engaged in, and because, presumably, the insatiably polygamous monarch was incapable of such wedded love. The three-character view, however, requires much reading between the lines. It rejects Solomon as the writer, though internal evidence as well as

tradition point to him as the author. We can explain references to
the shepherding and flocks as a metaphorical allusion to Solomon
as the leader of Israel, God's flock (cf. Num. 27:16, 17; Eze.
34:1ff.).

At first the lack of a readily recognizable story dismayed us.
No one thrills to a well-told story—or enjoys telling one—more
than Karen. And by "well-told" she means in detail, including
the color and fabric of the curtains at the windows and the pattern
of the wallpaper. I am more concerned about the facts and their
accuracy, and prefer not to discuss details if I'm not positive
about them. Karen, on the other hand, doesn't want to pass on a
dull story. For me, to say "sunset" is enough, but Karen's
mind's eye captures "that fleeting, magic moment when pink
cotton candy clouds bid adieu to their sky partner, the westward
sliding sun." Fellow lovers of stories and illustrations have her to
thank for their inclusion in these pages.

Two thoughts have helped us deal with the absence of either
detailed narrative or historically verifiable facts. First was the
profound way in which the Song, like the Bible as a whole, has
universal appeal. One of the family episodes in Scripture that we
frequently use in our marriage seminars is that of Isaac, Rebekah,
Jacob, and Esau found in Genesis 27. Often we assign individuals in our classes to read the various character parts. In
discussions afterward, we never cease to be amazed at how
people living centuries later and from all over the world so
readily discern the lessons from these ancient experiences.
Likewise with the Song of Songs. It describes a series of
authentic, intimate, personal portraits. Because they are not
highly detailed, readers can readily and universally identify with
them. To this extent it becomes, not only Solomon and Shulamith's song, but the song of every married couple. Further, the
principles of relational living inherent in it apply to all in close
relationships.

Reflecting on Wordsworth's claim that poets have an exceptional grasp of human emotions and feelings, we realized that the
Song of Songs exhibits the power of poetry. The ideas break
upon us, not so much through cognitive facts and ideas, but

through the senses. A poem transfuses emotions from the poet's
heart to ours.

The Hidden Structure of the Song

One of the delightful features of Hebrew poetry is the manner
in which it achieves rhyme through the use of parallelism, or
"thought rhyme." In the simplest form of parallelism, an
additional line or lines repeats the ideas of the first line(s) of the
verse, like a sound and its echo:

> You are all fair, my love,
>> And there is no spot in you (S. of Sol. 4:7).

> Behold, he comes
>> Leaping upon the mountains,
>>> Skipping upon the hills (S. of Sol. 2:8).

Occasionally, whole verses are in parallel (S. of Sol. 1:13,
14). Sometimes parallelism enlarges the thought (S. of Sol. 2:6),
or provides contrast (S. of Sol. 8:9). At times the poet constructs
a sequence of thoughts that he then echoes, but in reverse order,
with a mirror-like effect:

> Let me see your countenance,   a
>> Let me hear your voice;   b
> For your voice is sweet, b^1
>> And your countenance is lovely. a^1
>> (S. of Sol. 2:14).

Here the last two lines repeat the "countenance" and "voice" of
the earlier lines. This kind of reversing parallelism stretches over
several verses in Solomon's invitation to Shulamith (verses
2:10-13, TEV):

> Come then, my love; my darling, come with me.   a
>> The winter is over; the rains have stopped;   b
>> In the countryside the flowers are in bloom.
>>> This is the time for singing;   c
>
>> The song of doves is heard in the fields. c^1
>> Figs are beginning to ripen; b^1
>> The air is fragrant with blossoming vines.
> Come then, my love; my darling, come with me. a^1

The material follows the sequence $a:b:c:c^1:b^1:a^1$—invitation (a), description of spring (b), song/singing (c), song/singing (c^1), description of spring (b^1), invitation (a^1).

This more complex use of parallelism scholars term *chiasm*, a literary device similar to the picture created by a rainbow reflecting in a lake. As the colors of the rainbow appear in reverse order on the water's surface, so the segments on one side of the chiasm's intersection are generally arranged in reverse sequence to those of the opposite half. Corresponding sections show similar, though not necessarily identical, words or ideas. The intersecting point of the chiasm represents the hub or central statement and serves as an important key to understanding the meaning of the whole.

Recent studies have shown that the book forms an intricate chiasm:

CHIASTIC STRUCTURE OF THE SONG OF SOLOMON[2]

S. of Sol. 1:2-2:2   a
Wife's desire for her husband (1:2)
Solomon named (1:5)
"My own vineyard" (1:6)
Silver (1:11)
"My breasts" (1:13)
Evaluation of her (favorable) (1:15, 16)
Cedar (1:17)

S. of Sol. 2:3-17   b
The apple tree (2:3-5)
Charge to the Jerusalem girls (2:6, 7)
The beloved visits her home (2:8, 9)
His invitation to an outing (2:10-15)
Marriage covenant formula (2:16)

S. of Sol. 3:1-4:15   c
Dream I, search-encounter (3:1-4)
Charge to Jerusalem girls (3:5)
Praise of Solomon's procession (3:6-10)
Wedding scene (coronation of groom) (3:11)
Praise of bride's beauty and character (4:7-15)

S. of Sol. 4:16   d

Her invitation (4:16)

S. of Sol. 5:1 d^1
His response (5:1)

S. of Sol. 5:2-7:9 c^1
Dream II, encounter-search (5:2-7)
Charge to Jerusalem girls (5:8)
Praise of Solomon's person (5:9-6:3)
Praise of bride's character (6:4-10)
Wedding scene (dance of the bride) (6:11-13)
Praise of bride's beauty (7:1-9)

S. of Sol. 7:10-8:5 b^1
Marriage covenant formula (7:10)
Her invitation to an outing (7:11-13)
A wish that he might visit her home (8:1, 2)
Charge to Jerusalem girls (8:3, 4)
The apple tree (8:5)

S. of Sol. 8:6-14 a^1
Cedar (8:8, 9)
Evaluation of her (unfavorable) (8:8, 9)
"My breasts" (8:10)
Silver (8:11)
"My own vineyard" (8:12)
Solomon named (8:12)
Wife's desire for her husband (8:14)

This internal framework provides a valuable key to the meaning of the poem. It reveals a single, unified piece with remarkable literary artistry. The midpoint of the chiasm highlights the central theme of intimacy and oneness. Alone with his bride on their wedding night, Solomon compares her to a pleasant, fragrant, though locked garden (S. of Sol. 4:12-14). She invites her groom to come to the garden and partake of it. Solomon accepts her invitation. The two delicately crafted verses describing the consummation of their love (verse 16; 5:1) are the pivot of the great chiasm in the Song of Songs. They form the exact middle of the Hebrew text, with 111 Hebrew lines from 1:2 to 4:15, and 111 Hebrew lines from 5:2 to 8:14.

Further, the chiasm solves the problems raised by trying to tie the Song's episodes together chronologically, the most notable problem being the moral questions arising from her visiting the king's chambers (S. of Sol. 1:4), their sleeping together (verses 13, 16), and the intimate touching (S. of Sol. 2:6) all of which appear in the poem before the account of the wedding day (S. of Sol. 3:11-5:2). Other events appear after the references to the wedding night, though they occurred before it, such as the meeting of the two wedding parties (S. of Sol. 6:12, 13).

Finally, the mirror-imaging of the chiasm—its point and counterpoint, its two complementary parts making the whole—provide a literary device that corresponds with the relationship of the leading figures, Solomon and Shulamith, to each other in marriage. The governing structure of the poem itself complements the equality and mutuality that the Song proclaims.

Connecting Nature, Love, and God

Solomon's vast knowledge of the natural sciences appears in the numerous references to animals, plants, gardens, orchards, vineyards, spices, perfumes, and precious stones. The winsome way he presents nature lifts one's thoughts toward God, the Creator. The couple are not naive, though—the world in which they live is not sinless. Anger and injustice (S. of Sol. 1:6), foxes that spoil the vines (S. of Sol. 2:15), violence and pain (S. of Sol. 5:7), and death (S. of Sol. 8:6) have blighted Creation's fair face. But the man and woman sense at the same time that they live in the midst of something delightful. Frolicking in nature, they appreciate themselves and each other more by comparisons with it. Further, the Song declares that humanity—our relationships, our feelings, even our human bodies—are part of that creation. The attraction, the affection, the love the pair feels for each other, the delight they find in each other emotionally and physically, are just as good as the entire creation to them is good. It all is the doing of a good Creator.

---

[1] William Wordsworth, "Preface to the Second Edition of Several of the Foregoing Poems, Published, With an Additional Volume, Under the Title of Lyrical Ballads, 1800."

[2] Adapted from William H. Shea, "The Chiastic Structure of the Song of Songs." *Zeitschrift Für Die Alttestamentliche Wissenschaft*, ed. Georg Fohrer (New York: Walter De Gruyter, 1980), book 92, copy 3.

CHAPTER 4

Unraveling the Mystery of Solomon's Song

In the twelfth century A.D., Bernard of Clairvaux preached 86 sermons on the Song of Solomon. In Sermon 63, he devoted one entire message to the meaning of the "teeth" of S. of Sol. 4:2, proclaiming with amazing flourish:

"As the teeth are whiter than the rest of the body, so the Religious are the purest members of the Church. . . . As the teeth are cloistered by the lips, so are the Religious cloistered by the walls of the convent. . . . The teeth do not taste the dainties they chew, and so the Religious take no credit for the good they do. Teeth do not easily decay and perseverance is a quality of the cloistered life. They are ranked in fixed and even order, and nowhere is there such orderliness as in the convent. There are upper and lower teeth, so the monasteries have dignitaries and ordinary members united in harmonious toil. When the lower teeth move, the uppers remain still, denoting the calmness with which Superiors should rule, even where there is commotion in the lower ranks of the community. . . . The teeth of the Bride are compared to shorn sheep, the shearings being innocent meditations, which cut away the outer things, such as love of earth and desire for worldly wisdom. They come up from the washing of compunction and penitential tears. . . . They produce twins because they develop both contemplation and action, or teach by precept and example.'' [1]

Bernard interpreted the Song of Songs as an allegory, bestowing symbolic meaning on every word and phrase as he went along. In so doing, he was following in the longstanding tradition of many scholars both in Judaism and in the early church. In the tenth century Jewish scholar Saadia ben Joseph reflected on a millennium of such an approach as he began his own commentary. ''You will find great differences in interpretation of the Song of Songs. In truth they differ because the Song of Songs resembles locks to which the keys have been lost.'' [2]

Detour Into Dualism

The allegorical method of interpretation has its roots in ancient Hellenistic Greek philosophy with its dualism of body and spirit, which simply meant that things relating to the physical body and its needs were bad and hindered the growth of the Spirit. The most worthy quest of life, Hellenistic Greeks reasoned, was to free the spirit from the contamination of the earthly, lustful body. Such a belief led intellectuals like Plato to feel the need to reinterpret the carnal passions of Zeus and other deities of early Greek mythology whose gross immoral conduct proved an embarrassment to the Stoics at the very least, if not actually undermining their most cherished beliefs. Through the use of allegory, he explained away the unacceptable conduct of the gods as not being their actual behavior but as having symbolic meaning, thus bringing it more into line with the enlightened Stoic ideal of distancing humanity from all fleshly passion. Allegory deliberately bypassed the literal meaning. The simple sense of the literature (which made them uncomfortable) they invested with a hidden meaning that they felt to be more appropriate.

During the centuries just before the time of Christ, as Jewish scholars in Alexandria, Egypt, imbibed the Hellenist philosophy around them, they retooled the simple straightforward interpretation of the Song of Solomon and in time replaced its plain meaning by allegory. What began as a valid use of the Song to illustrate Jehovah's love for Israel eventually became almost an elaborate game in which scholars interpreted the words of the

Song to describe in lavish detail the history of Israel from the Exodus to the Exile.

"The verse 'A sachet of myrrh is my beloved to me, Between my breasts it lies' (1:13) was found by Rashi and Ibn Ezra to be a reference to the Shekinah, between the cherubim that stood over the Ark. . . . 'On my bed by night I sought him whom my soul loveth, I sought him but I found him not' (3:1) referred to the years of wandering in the wilderness. . . . 'Black am I but comely, O daughters of Jerusalem' (1:5) was taken to mean that Israel was black by reason of the making of the Golden Calf, but comely by reason of receiving the Ten Commandments." [3]

Tradition says that at Jamnia, not far from what is now Tel Aviv, Jewish scholars met in 90 A.D. to consider whether the Song of Solomon should become a permanent part of the Hebrew Bible. Rabbi Akiba, who pioneered in the development of the Song as a history of Israel, secured its place with a persuasive speech: "The whole world is not worth the day on which the Song of Songs was given to Israel, for all the Scriptures are holy, but the Song of Songs is the Holy of Holies." Elsewhere Akiba reportedly said, "Had not the Torah been given, Canticles would have sufficed to guide the world." [4]

Thus interpreted, the Song of Songs came to be read at Passover. It was inserted in the Hebrew Bible as the first of the Five Scrolls of the Writings (Song of Solomon, Ruth, Lamentations, Ecclesiastes, Esther), corresponding to the sequence of their use in the round of Jewish holy days.

When Christianity advanced westward from Palestine into the Hellenistic-Roman world, the church, like Judaism before it, found itself influenced by its surroundings. Some early Church Fathers sought to establish common ground between Christianity and the people they were trying to reach. Origen of Alexandria (third century A.D.) fully embraced Plato's philosophy of the opposing types—the earthly/physical versus the heavenly/spiritual. Regarding Song of Solomon 1:4 he wrote, "There is a love of the flesh which comes from Satan, and there is also another love, belonging to the Spirit, which has its origin in God; and nobody can be possessed by the two loves. . . . If you have despised all bodily things . . . then you can acquire spiritual love." Elsewhere in his 12-volume commentary on the Song of Solomon, which would shape the thinking of much of Christendom ever after, he said, "I advise and counsel everyone who is not yet rid of the vexations of flesh and blood and has not ceased to feel the passion of his bodily nature, to refrain completely from reading this little book and the things that will be said about it." [5]

Origen transformed Jewish allegory of the Song, which he knew well, into Christian terms. "Black am I but comely, O daughters of Jerusalem" (S. of Sol. 1:5) meant black with sin but comely through conversion.[6] Mistakenly thinking that the bridegroom spoke Song of Solomon 2:1, he saw in the two flowers a reference to the gospel going to the Gentiles. Christ was first the Rose of Sharon (the cultivated plain of Sharon he believed stood for the Jews), and then the Lily of the valleys (the rocky, untilled soil of the valleys representing the Gentiles).[7] In Song of Solomon 6:8, "Origen saw the queens as the perfect souls, the concubines those who are progressing, and the virgins those who are just beginning on the way to perfection." [8]

"Philo Carpasius and Cyril of Alexandria believed 'A sachet of myrrh is my beloved to me, Between my breasts it lies' (1:13) to refer to the Scriptures of the Old and New Testaments, between which stands Christ. . . . Cyril of Jerusalem saw in the words 'King Solomon made himself a palanquin' (3:9) a reference to the Cross, and in its 'silver pillars' an allusion to Judas's thirty pieces of silver, and in 'the crown wherewith his mother crowned him in the day of his espousals' a reference to the crown of thorns." [9]

For centuries the allegorical method has left the Song open to any interpretation the imagination of its expositors could devise. In addition to the typical interpretation by Jews and Christians, some consider it to be an allegory of the love of the pagan god Tammuz for the goddess Ishtar. For some Roman Catholics, the bride is the virgin Mary. Martin Luther saw in the poem Solomon's praise for his people's loyalty, the bride symbolizing the state. In addition to a history of the past, some have even seen in it a prophecy of the future.

Christ and the Song of Solomon

"Oh, that's about Christ and the church," a friend exclaimed when we announced our intention to write a book about the Song of Solomon. "Well, yes and no," we replied, sharing a little of what we had learned.

No doubt allegorical preaching, teaching, writing, and even singing (e.g., "He's the Lily of the Valley," "His banner over us is love") have blessed many. But to the extent that allegorical interpretation reflects the errors inherent in the Greek philosophy of dualism of body and spirit, it will continue to divert attention from the plain sense of the Song and its full message.

Scholar Marvin Pope, after devouring countless volumes of allegory on the Song, concludes:

"The flexibility and adaptability of the allegorical method, the ingenuity and the imagination with which it could be, and was, applied, the difficulty and virtual impossibility of imposing objective controls, the astounding and bewildering results of almost two millennia of application of the Canticle, have all contributed to its progressive discredit and almost complete desertion." [10]

Some offer the Song as a *typology*, i.e., the husband is a *type* of Christ and the wife a *type* of the church or the individual believer. Typology accepts the validity of the literal account, but thinks of it as foreshadowing some greater reality that will ultimately replace or supersede the historical or literal sense. Nowhere, however, does Scripture speak of human marriage as a type to be replaced, as, say, the earthly sanctuary that represented Christ's ministry was replaced.

Further, typology tends to take the focus off the type rather quickly in order to teach about the antitype. We believe God placed the book within Scripture to teach about human relationships. Individuals and families seeking to understand and follow the divine plan need its truths. Its validity as a book about human relationship will endure as long as people and families need guidance.

Viewing Solomon as a type of Christ raises a number of problems. Alongside the idealism of marriage and the joy of being together that the couple share, we find hints of his inconstancy. Her appeal for time, attention, and an exclusive relationship with him (S. of Sol. 1:7) imply that he is less than perfect, as do her frightening dreams of losing him (S. of Sol. 3:1-4; 5:2-7) and her persistent appeal for a permanent covenant with him (S. of Sol. 8:6, 7).

An illustration of divine love. The late professor John Murray, a Reformed theologian who long espoused the allegorical approach to the Song, reached a most reasonable conclusion about the Song and its relationship to Christ.

"I cannot now endorse the allegorical interpretation of the Song of Solomon. I think the vagaries of interpretation given in terms of the allegorical principle indicate that there are no well-defined hermeneutical canons to guide us in determining the precise meaning and application if we adopt the allegorical view. However, I also think that in terms of the biblical analogy the Song could be used to *illustrate* the relation of Christ to His church. The marriage bond is used in Scripture as a pattern of Christ and the church. If the Song portrays marital love and relationship on the highest levels of exercise and devotion, then surely it may be used to exemplify what is transcendently true in the bond that exists between Christ and the church." [11]

We have had the privilege of tasting many of the world's cuisines in their local settings. Were we to compare a new flavor for you to the taste of snake fruit, one of our favorite delicacies from Indonesia, you would probably not understand the comparison unless you too had visited Indonesia. So the illustrative value of the Song of Songs relies upon our experience of human love.

The Missing Key

We find the key to unlock the mystery of the Song of Solomon in the Bible's own wholistic view of the nature of humankind. The biblical record states of the creation of human beings, "And the Lord God formed man of the dust of the ground, and breathed into his nostrils the breath of life, and man became a living being" (Gen. 2:7). Here the Hebrew term *nephesh*, "soul" (KJV), describes the whole person, not just a part of him or her. The individual does not *have* a soul—rather, he or she *is* a soul.

"It must . . . be realized that in the Biblical faith, there is

never any split made between the material and spiritual worlds.
. . . In the Biblical view, human beings are always considered as
psychophysical wholes. They cannot be split into separate parts
of soul and body, mind and spirit.''[12]

The two Creation accounts portray the human body and its
sexual characteristics as a good gift of God (Gen. 1:27, 31;
2:23-25). The prophets confirm the Bible's wholesome and
positive attitude toward human sexuality through their inspired
use of marital intimacy to describe God's relationship with His
people (Isa. 54:5; 62:4, 5; Jer. 3:14; Eze. 16:8). In the section of
the Hebrew scriptures known as the Writings, we find further
indications of a positive attitude toward the human body. When
the psalmist hungers for fellowship with God, it is with his flesh
as well as with his spirit (Ps. 63:1; 84:1, 2). Nor does the Bible
blush to speak openly of the body and its sexual attractiveness
(Prov. 5:15-19; S. of Sol. 7:1-10).

After the entrance of sin, human nature was no longer
flawless. The centuries since have progressively marred and
dimmed the image of God in man. While our human love and
sexuality is no longer perfect, sin did not cause God to abandon
His design. Rather the gospel seeks to recover the soul and ''to
retrace upon it His own image in righteousness and holiness.'' [13]
In the New Testament Christ's redemption of persons includes
the redemption of the body. ''Glorify God in your body and in
your spirit, which are God's'' (1 Cor. 6:20).

Major Symbols of the Song

In the Song, the mysteries of married love, of human bonding
and sexuality, open to us with the gracefulness of an unfolding
blossom. Similes and metaphors abound: ''I have compared you,
my love, to my filly among Pharaoh's chariots'' (S. of Sol. 1:9);
''Like an apple tree . . . , so is my beloved among the sons'' (S.
of Sol. 2:3); ''A bundle of myrrh is my beloved to me'' (S. of
Sol. 1:13); ''A garden enclosed is my sister, my spouse'' (S. of
Sol. 4:12). An important principle in their interpretation, as in all
of Scripture, is to look for the most natural, reasonable sense.
Regardless of the levels of meaning that we may draw from them
for illustration or devotional purposes, faithfulness to the Scrip-

ture requires that we consider the most obvious, the most easily understood meaning for the first readers of the text. Other uses in Scripture, the context surrounding the symbols, and the emotion conveyed by the symbols all provide clues to their meaning.

A brief look at a few of the major symbols will enable us to grasp more easily the intent of the Song. As we seek to unlock the metaphors, we need to remember that God had reasons for veiling the Song thus. As in the parables of Jesus, the Song contains truths that the people were unprepared to understand, let alone accept. Yet Christ offered them with care and sensitivity for custom and culture, knowing that as the meaning dawned in the minds of His hearers some would scorn it, but others would cherish what they now grasped. So in the Song. The book describes the delicate scenes of wedded love with the language of poetry and the imagery of metaphor so as not to create awkwardness or embarrassment or evoke negative reactions, but rather to invite us to cherish and enjoy God's good gift.

Vineyard. Shulamith speaks of her vineyard (S. of Sol. 1:6). While she may have owned a literal vineyard, the allusion seeks to communicate something more. The context reveals her concern about her swarthy complexion and parallels her statement about her own vineyard having gone unattended. The Song often plays upon double meanings, and here it introduces its leading double entendre. The vineyard symbolizes the woman herself, then broadens to become a garden paradise with fragrant plants and shrubs, exotic fruits, and refreshing fountains (S. of Sol. 4:12-5:1).

Although first showing her uneasiness and perhaps some anxiety about her personal worth, at the end of the poem the metaphor reappears in a manner that suggests that she now has a healthy self-assurance and sense of autonomy. "My own vineyard is mine to give" (S. of Sol. 8:12, NIV). In contrast to the leased plantation of Solomon in Baal Hamon, there is no shareholding with her. Her "vineyard" is her gift to him. Symbolically speaking, he not only receives the income from the lease, but gets the fruit also. Nor does he pay wages to fruit-tenders, since he himself is the fruit-tender of this vineyard (compare S. of Sol. 4:13, 16; 7:13).

Lily. Shulamith calls herself a rose of Sharon, a lily of the

valleys (S. of Sol. 2:1). Both the grammar and context indicate
that they are her words. The flowers to which she compares
herself are the simple, common wildflowers of Palestine. Her
identification of herself as a lily reveals another of the Song's
symbols for the woman, and provides a key to interpretation of
later verses (compare S. of Sol. 2:16; 4:5; 6:3).

Gazelle. The book compares Solomon to a gazelle (S. of Sol.
2:9), beautiful, graceful animals that hint at the physical charms
and attributes of her spouse (Compare Prov. 5:19; S. of Sol. 2:7,
16, 17; 3:5; 6:3; 8:14). The allusion helps us to understand the
meaning of "he feeds . . . among the lilies" (S. of Sol. 2:16;
compare S. of Sol. 6:2, 3). The Hebrew word "feed" may
indicate either feeding someone, something, or oneself. Feeding
oneself fits the context best here. The words "his flocks" are not
in the Hebrew but have been supplied. In the symbols of the
Song, Shulamith is a lily and her beloved a gazelle. Her husband
is a caring companion, one she trusts, one to whom she has
opened her life. To her he is not a marauding fox, wantonly and
ravagingly spoiling the tender grapes (S. of Sol. 2:15), but is a
gentle gazelle who "browses" (verse 16, NIV), taking emotional
and physical delight in her.

Mountain. "Be like a gazelle . . . upon the mountains of
Bether" (verse 17), Shulamith invites Solomon. Some have
interpreted the phrase as her bidding her beloved farewell as he
returns over the rugged hills after his springtime visit (verse 8).
However, no such geographical mountains are known. "Bether"
derives from a root word meaning "to cut in two," hence
possibly "cleft mountains." [14] Since the book employs objects
of nature elsewhere as subtle symbols for its characters, it is
probably most in harmony with the context to see in the cleft
mountains a figurative reference to the lady herself. The verse is
her invitation, delicately veiled, for her husband to enjoy a time
of intimacy with her.

The Song further develops the mountain motif as a symbol of
the woman and her charms in Song of Solomon 4:6 ("mountain
of myrrh," "hill of frankincense"), 4:8, and 8:14. Just as
Solomon's delight in horses provided a comparison to her (S. of
Sol. 1:9), so now he uses his pleasure with this mountainous

region's scenic grandeur (S. of Sol. 4:8), the fresh fragrance of its vegetation and forests (verse 11), and the refreshing quality of its waters (verse 15) to describe her qualities. She becomes a personification of Lebanon. When he invites, "Come with me from Lebanon," it may be an echoing of his first invitation with which he once wooed and won her, and with which he now invites her to the most intimate act of marriage.

An Inside Look at a Good Marriage

The newsstands and media lend credence to the sad stories of scores of couples who have moved in and out of our lives for whom the experience of marriage has been an unfulfilling, disappointing, even bitter one. Many have never been married at all. We might expect, therefore, that our all-wise God would give some inside look at the bonds of affection in a good marriage in His Word. Seeing it demonstrated in Scripture might be the only positive example some would have, but having it available here to read over and over again would be for all a continuing source of hope, inspiration, and instruction. Such a display of marital love and intimacy would also serve to exemplify on a human level the bond that exists between Christ and His Church. This insightful model of marital love the Song of Solomon provides.

---

[1] Marvin H. Pope, *Song of Songs* (New York: Doubleday, 1977), p. 463.

[2] *Ibid.*, p. 89.

[3] H. H. Rowley, "The Interpretation of the Song of Songs," *The Servant of the Lord and Other Essays on the Old Testament* (Oxford: Basil Blackwell & Mott Ltd., 1965), pp. 200, 201.

[4] Pope, p. 92.

[5] *Ibid.*, pp. 115, 117.

[6] Rowley, pp. 203, 204.

[7] Pope, pp. 369, 370.

[8] *Ibid.*, p. 569.

[9] Rowley, pp. 203, 204.

[10] Pope, p. 90.

[11] G. Lloyd Carr, *The Song of Solomon* (Downers Grove, Ill.: InterVarsity Press), p. 23.

[12] Elizabeth Achtemeier, *The Committed Marriage* (Philadelphia: Westminster Press, 1976), p. 157.

[13] Ellen G. White, *Christ's Object Lessons* (Washington, D.C.: Review and Herald Pub. Assn., 1941), p. 194.

[14] *The Seventh-day Adventist Bible Commentary* (Washington, D.C.: Review and Herald Pub. Assn., 1953), vol. 3, p. 1116.

CHAPTER 5

Quests of the Heart

S hulamith's kinship with us all is quickly apparent in the poem. Her opening lines reflect briefly on three episodes of their married life at the palace. While she speaks frankly of her desire for his physical attention, it is but a part of the longing. Like every man and woman who has ever lived, she seeks affirmation of her personhood by a loved one and acceptance for who she is, despite her imperfections.

Reflections of a Longing Heart

Solomon has truly captured the hearts of his people. In the first vignette or scene of the poem (S. of Sol. 1:2-4), Shulamith both rejoices in his popularity and finds it cause for concern. His admirers include women—beautiful women—and their obvious love and admiration for their monarch naturally makes her crave reassurance that while he loves all his subjects as a good king should, she alone holds the keys to the innermost chambers of his heart. She needs to know that for him she is enough.

The second keyhole glimpse into the life of Shulamith at the palace (verses 5, 6) frames her in the company of her attendants, the daughters of Jerusalem. The book of Esther with its allusion to the beauty regimens common to women of the ancient Near Eastern court can perhaps help us picture the scene more fully.

Shulamith feels the eyes of the others upon her. The hue of her
skin, her dress, her hair, her accent, her mannerisms—everything
about her sets her apart, just when she would so like to fit in and
be like the others. Women quickly pick up on their culture's
expectations for beauty and charm, and Shulamith is no exception. But such knowledge inevitably produces an uncomfortable
awareness of her personal flaws.

The third glimpse into their life together has been complicated by translators who may have missed some of the Song's
veiled metaphor. In Song of Solomon 1:7 Shulamith asks
Solomon, "Where do you feed?" (The words "your flock" are
not in the original text, but have been supplied by modern
translators.) The real intent of her question becomes clearer as
she continues, "Why should I be as one who veils herself by the
flocks of your companions?" Solomon is not actually a shepherd,
of course, though as we have seen, the shepherd metaphor is a
common one for the leaders of God's people. Rather the passage
introduces another of the Song's double meanings. Here Shulamith, in a moment of anxiety, seeks assurance that she is first in
Solomon's affections, both physically and emotionally. She does
not want to have to pursue him for his love as a prostitute ("one
veiled") solicits a man. While her attendants see nothing wrong
with her seeking after him (they advise her to "follow in the
footsteps of the flock"), Shulamith implies by the use of this
imagery that she feels demeaned by his lack of attention.

The force of the prostitute simile may indicate a setting later
in their marriage when Solomon's affections may have begun to
wander. The use of random flashback in the overall creation of
the chiastic structure of the poem allows for the vignettes to come
from different seasons in their marriage. But Shulamith's under-
lying concern in all three scenes is the same: "Am I valued as a
person?" In her expression of this fundamental human need for
personal worth, she reveals herself as a bona fide representative
of the human race. And in seeking evidence of her worth
primarily in the context of human relationships she stands with
women the world over.

Solomon does not as openly express his need for personal
worth. Perhaps it is because men typically do not expose their

need as readily, perhaps because he is not even consciously aware of it. After all, he is the king, one who by virtue of his position, if nothing else, receives an inordinate amount of affirmation and acclaim. Then, too, he is youthful, handsome, rich, talented, gifted intellectually—well endowed with all the traits societies everywhere have always valued. But the subtle evidence indicated by his wandering affections reveals the depth of his need. He too seeks answers to the same question, but only in his old age does he realize he has been searching in all the wrong places.

Not long ago I returned to Andrews Academy for the twenty-fifth reunion of my academy class. All but five of my classmates attended, and I found myself wishing I could be both a participant and an observer of an event that proved later to defy description as I tried to tell Ron about it. Friday evening found us gathered in the family room of a classmate still living in our home town, chattering like teenagers, still competing for attention, seemingly having to reenter one another's lives exactly where we had left off two and a half decades before. That weekend we spent close to 30 hours with each other. We laughed at old yearbook advice that bordered on the prophetic—"When you get old and out of shape, remember girdles cost $2.98!" and shared the good things that had happened, both then and since. It was only in the wee hours of Sunday morning that we began to settle into what George Eliot called "the indescribable comfort" of friendship that allowed us to feel safe with one another, daring to hope that each would take us as we really are, "chaff and grain together . . . keeping what is worth keeping, and with a breath of kindness, blow the rest away." [1]

The inadequacies we felt so keenly during our teenage years linger with many of us for a lifetime. As I sat among my classmates, studying their faces, memory after memory flashed through my mind. I had longed to be pretty like Wanda, shapely like Hilda, popular like Georgene, smart like Kathy, witty like Joe and Roger. Even now the longings had not totally vanished, though they'd been eased considerably by a growing understanding of the gospel, compensating fulfillments, and the warmth and security of relationships waiting for me at home.

Handiwork of the Eternal I AM

While the Bible does not speak directly of self-worth or low self-esteem, it addresses the issue at the foundational level. In the beginning, fresh from the Creator's hand, the first man and woman knew nothing of the struggle for a sense of personal worth that has now reached epidemic proportions in our world. In Eden, both male and female understood themselves in relation to their Creator. Their worth was a bestowed one, rooted deeply in the sovereignty and goodness of the God in whose likeness they had been created. They were who they were because of who He is, protecting them from all that would degrade them on the one hand, and all that would seek to elevate them to the status of gods or centers of absolute power on the other. And the ideals upon which they built their relationship with each other emanated from this primary relationship and all that it implied.

Secure in the knowledge that they were persons of inestimable value because they were the handiwork of the eternal I AM, the Bible says the first human beings knew no shame (Gen. 2:25). In their unfallen state, the absence of shame (the root condition that creates low self-worth) meant simply that in their relationship to God, they were content with their creatureliness. As individual human beings, it was good to be male and it was good to be female. God had said so, and that was enough. And in relationship to each other, they could be "naked and unashamed," symbolizing the openness and honesty they knew between them. They could be their true, authentic selves in each other's presence with nothing to hide and no walls to separate.

The Emergence of Shame

But, enticed by the idea that they might become more than human, even like God Himself, our first parents found themselves lured into dissatisfaction with their creatureliness. The Bible records that among the tragedies that their transgression brought in its wake were a fear of exposure and a discomfort with their nakedness. They now knew shame. It no longer felt good to be who they were. And so they gathered fig leaves about themselves and went into hiding. In truth, the human family, driven by shame, have engaged in a perplexing assortment of behaviors ever since, seeking to "hide" themselves from God and from each other.

The first shame known by human beings, with its accompanying feelings of guilt and low self-worth, resulted from disobedience. All of us today experience the condemning shame of our first parents to some extent because it comes part and parcel with being "in Adam," with the sinful condition into which each member of the human race is now born. We add to our pathetic legacy by committing our own transgressions. But God, who continually works good out of bad, uses the guilt and shame arising from our sinful condition and our own willful disobedience to lead us both to an understanding of our fallenness and to repentance. Satan, however, often manipulates our sense of shame to draw us into a dark valley of self-condemnation that knows no forgiveness, no self-acceptance, no inner peace.

The shame-reinforcing experiences we encounter from childhood on further compound our problem. Prayer meeting was nearly half over when the back door of the church swung slowly open and a tall young man dressed in army fatigues slipped into the back pew. After saying good night to the last of the church members, we turned our attention to the strange man waiting awkwardly in the back of the sanctuary. He had come to our city to find work, he said. But he was running short of cash and needed some money for a place to stay the night and a little food. Having more of ourselves than money to give, we took him home with us. After a warm shower, some hot soup, and a sandwich, he began to relax and to unfold his story.

Bud had never done well in school. Although he'd tried, he guessed school just wasn't for him. It took him until he was 16 to get through the eighth grade, so against his parents' wishes, he quit school, left home, lied about his age, and joined the Army. He had been reared in the church tradition of conscientious objector status, but he so wanted to fit in with the other recruits that he reluctantly took up weapons training.

One night, while assigned to patrol in a combat zone, he came face to face with the enemy—another mere lad like himself. The two so frightened and unnerved each other that both turned and ran in opposite directions. But not without someone observing and reporting it to the commanding officer. Bud received a dishonorable discharge. Back home, he married, but the relationship faced major problems from the beginning. A new baby coincided with a failed business, and all in all, it proved too much. And so, broken both in pocket and spirit, he had followed the thin shaft of light that connected the cold street corner to the church door.

Bud stayed with us several days, but jobs were scarce and discouragement disabling. One morning after breakfast he left. I fear the best we had to offer then were the memory of a few days of warmth, an ample lunch, money for a bus ticket back home, and a prayer that God might meet his need. We never saw him again, but I can't help wishing he might read this book. For we have come to understand many things since then.

Many of us have been spared the magnitude of shame-reinforcing experiences the Buds among us have known. Others know pain that runs much deeper. Even the church is no stranger to abuse. Millions suffer the rest of their lives because of the destructive abuse they received from parents or other adults entrusted with their care. Still others agonize at work, at school, in the church, or at home. Many know the searing pain of spouse abuse despite covenants to love, honor, and cherish.

We are all victims to one degree or another. Whether we're not thin enough, or muscular enough, or smart enough, or rich enough, or outstanding enough at whatever is in vogue, we feel shamed to the degree that we cannot measure up to society's standards. Others of us have been the victims of a toxic faith. We have borne the shame arising from a faulty theology that demands human striving and perfection in exchange for the assurance of salvation. A faith that leaves uncondemned only those who fool themselves. A belief that blurs the distinction between our full justification in Jesus Christ alone and God's call to holy living and the work He does in us as His already saved children.

Both of us grew up in cold climes. Ron's home turf is New Brunswick, Canada, where the winters are long and hard. Dad Flowers spent much of his life as a carpenter and builder. In that part of the world every builder knows to bury water pipes at least six feet deep so they will not freeze, for constant tramping on the surface forces the fingers of frost farther and farther down into the ground. In a similar manner, life's experiences can drive shame so deeply into us that it becomes our permanent condition. Shame is then no longer merely a consequence of our fallenness, but rather takes over our identity, leaving us feeling flawed and defective. Only with great difficulty will we then be able to accept God's forgiveness and the value He bestows upon us, and to forgive ourselves and feel good about who we are in Christ.

The apostle refers to this problem when he speaks in 1 John 3:20 of our own hearts condemning us. Condemning shame haunts people of every nation, kindred, and tongue with the question "Am I a valuable person?" And the answer we give profoundly affects our personal lives and families. Such shame can not only control our own lives (as the wise man observed, "as a man thinks in his heart, so is he" [Prov. 23:7]), but also create enormous barriers to closeness in any type of relationship. We find it difficult to let others get close to us when we feel flawed and defective inside. Shame causes us to feel unworthy of both God's love and that of fellow human beings, and we fear that if anyone ever discovers what we are really like, that person will consider us unlovable.

We once asked a group of juniors in Vacation Bible School how they could tell when their friends didn't feel very good about themselves. They came up with a pretty perceptive list of evidence: they fight, put others down to build themselves up, take drugs, run away, act silly, don't make friends, go off by themselves, chew their nails, try to dress better than anyone else, don't do their homework, don't care about anything, get real fat, talk a lot to their friends but not to their parents, and get into trouble.

In truth, we as "grown-up children" also don subtle cover-up garments to hide our real selves from others because we are convinced that no one could love and accept us as we actually are. Such garments include perfectionism, striving for power and control, rage, self-sufficiency, arrogance, a critical spirit, judgmental attitudes, a fetish for pleasing and taking care of people, envy, and the full range of compulsive and addictive behaviors. Though they represent a baffling array of seemingly unrelated behaviors, all indicate the same inner malady—shame that creates low self-worth.

The Healer for Shame

Our families find themselves caught in the vicious downward spiral of being shamed and shaming in return that has enmeshed all generations since Adam. But because of Jesus Christ we can know with surety the true answer to the question "Am I a valuable person?"

The news was good from the beginning. God first proclaimed it when He called His erring children out of hiding in Eden. Instead of censure and condemnation, the "Where are you? Who told you you were naked? What have you done?" of Genesis 3 actually echoes God's passionate plea of Hosea 11:8, 9:

"How can I give you up, Ephraim?
How can I hand you over Israel? . . .
My heart churns within Me;
My sympathy is stirred. I will not execute the fierceness of My
    anger. . . .
For I am God and not man,
The Holy One in your midst."

It is the heart cry of One who weeps over His beloved city: "O Jerusalem, Jerusalem. . . . How often I wanted to gather your children together, as a hen gathers her chicks under her wings, but you were not willing!" (Matt. 23:37). It's invitation is repeated in the summons, "Come to me all you who labor and are heavy laden and I will give you rest" (Matt. 11:28). For the same Jesus whom Genesis 3 promises will bruise the serpent's head has since come to break down the dividing walls that separate us from God and from each other (cf. Eph. 2:14). The call of God still beckons, and the good news resounds as cause for great celebration.

Despite all that sin has done to mar God's image in us, every man, woman, and child alive bears His inscription still. Like the shepherd who missed one sheep or the woman who lost her coin, so the Son of God came to seek the lost because we are still of inestimable worth in His eyes.

All this was true before Calvary. But in the shadow of the cross, the good news is that Christ took upon Himself our shame. The cross upon which they crucified Christ was an instrument of humiliation and shame, but Jesus endured it, "disregarding its shame" (Heb. 12:2, NRSV). He took with Him to the cross the legacy of shame we have inherited "in Adam," the shame we have brought upon ourselves by our deliberate acts of sin, and all the shame heaped upon us by others. Christ bore the mocking and rejection, the fear of nakedness and exposure, the feelings of helplessness, loneliness, and abandonment. There, with the desperate cry "My God, my God, why hast thou forsaken me?" on His lips, He died the death that should have been ours (Matt. 27:46, KJV).

What are you worth? Contemplate the sacrifice made for you at Calvary and all that God has accomplished for you "in Christ."

"But now in Christ Jesus you who once were far off have been brought near by the blood of Christ" (Eph. 2:13).

"For He [God] made Him who knew no sin to be sin for us, that we might become the righteousness of God in Him" (2 Cor. 5:21).

"Through one man sin entered the world, and death [and shame] through sin . . . But where sin [and shame] abounded, grace abounded much more" (Romans 5:12-20).

"There is therefore now no condemnation to those who are in Christ Jesus" (Romans 8:1).

The paradox of the gospel is that God calls us out of our shameful hiding only to hide us again in the folds of Christ's garment of righteousness. In the exchange, He replaces the flimsy, tattered, see-through fig-leaf garments which we use to cover our shame with the perfect, seamless, all-sufficient robe of Christ's righteous life that has no taint of shame. The cross forever secured the good news that when we are "in Him," we are "accepted in the Beloved" (Eph. 1:6), once again God's children "in whom [He is] well pleased" (Matt. 3:17). It is an objective, unchangeable fact that we must cling to when Satan tries to overwhelm us with our sin and causes us to despair of our value. Even in the dark moments of self-condemnation we can rejoice, ''For if our heart condemns us, God is greater than our heart'' (1 John 3:20).

CHAPTER 6

A Healing Atmosphere

Theirs was a fabled romance. The young Robert Browning returned from the Continent to find England astir over a new edition of Miss Elizabeth Barrett's *Poems*. The poet-playwright was an adventurous, much-traveled bachelor, the poetess a fragile spinster sealed away from the rest of the world by a domineering father and her own ill health.

Although a porcelain glaze of propriety glossed every page of the letters that passed between them, deep admiration and growing devotion created warm hues beneath the surface. In time he ventured, "I love you," and pleaded to visit her. She pulled instinctively away, warning that "her poetry is the best of her." [1] "It has all my colours," she wrote. "The rest of me is nothing but a root, fit for the ground and the dark." [2] But love persisted, and Elizabeth slowly surrendered to it.

From childhood, she disclosed in her letter of November 12, 1845, she had hungered for an "irrational" love, for she could not imagine herself worthy of any other kind.[3] To find herself loved apart from pity for her condition or admiration for her genius was "something . . . between dream and miracle," [4] but she flourished under Robert's influence.

Many secrets lurked behind the red-brick front of the Barrett residence at 50 Wimpole Street. Mrs. Barrett was dead, the doors to her rooms locked the day of her death by a single command from her husband, who forbade the mention of her name from that day forward. Mr. Barrett, from all outward appearances a devoutly religious man, rigidly controlled his family and demanded obedience in the name of biblical authority. It was a household that tiptoed about his overpowering presence, fearful of touching one of his "vibratory wires" and setting off the rocking tremors of his explosive anger and his punitive wrath. "Oh, we understand in this house," [5] Elizabeth confided bitterly to Robert as she explained about the heavy emotional payment that Mr. Barrett would surely exact if Browning or anyone brushed him the wrong way.

Elizabeth was one of only three of his twelve children who ever dared defy him and marry. It was a decision for which her father and her brothers, except for George, would punish her for the rest of her life. Even the news of her father's death brought the mixed emotions of grief and relief, for though a family friend reported that he had in the end "forgiven" his married children, even prayed for their well-being, tragically it was only in the hearsay of his prayer life that he ever acknowledged their existence once they challenged his ultimate authority.

Elizabeth did not make her decision to marry without fear and trembling. Her inner turmoil reflected not only trouble with her father, but also her ongoing battle with shame. She once admitted that she had toyed with the idea of letting Robert "try me for one winter," [6] then offering to walk out of his life forever if she proved a disappointment. On another occasion she considered that perhaps she "should choose to die this winter—now—before I had disappointed you in anything." [7]

For Robert, the decision had been simpler. "What I mean by marrying you," he concluded in his letter of August 3, 1846, "it is, that I may be with you forever—I cannot have enough of you in any other relation." [8] She tells him he is blind, but for now she would accept his blindness. Having searched the length and breadth of Robert's devotion for hidden cracks and chinks, she eventually succumbed completely to an unconditional love that had at last "conquered fear, or worn it out." [9]

In response to our quest for personal worth and healing from the brokenness that shame has wreaked upon the human family for generations, God offers first the good news about Himself and the value He bestows upon each of us as His creation and as His sons and daughters "in Christ." It is the best news ever to reach humanity's ears, good news as unchangeable as the God who is its essence. And its proclamation brings healing on its wings.

But God uses human instruments to fully orchestrate the symphony of His love. Without the love of friends and family, the chords of divine love seem at times to play only in the distance, and the ear must strain to catch the full score. For as surely as divine love is the ultimate reality, so human love helps us to experience and know the divine. To love and be loved in the circle of family and friends is God's intended balm for the ravages of shame, His chosen means for bringing to every man, woman, and child the soothing touch of His grace.

Scripture preserves for us the true life experiences of men and women who brought God near to earth by their caring ministry to others threatened by the tidal wave of shame. For Naomi, there was Ruth. Naomi, in the space of one short decade, had faced the trauma of economic hardship and famine; a desperate move to a land disdained by all Israel with a different language and strange customs; the untimely death of her husband; the overload of rearing two sons alone; the anguish of seeing those sons marry outside her religion; their premature death; the encroachment of old age and its vanishing options; and finally the return to Bethlehem. There she had to brave the prospect of having to rehearse her sad tale for self-righteous townspeople likely thinking, *We told you so . . .* —to say nothing of an uncertain future without blood relative, without heir, without income.

"Do not call me Naomi," she held them at a distance, for the name Naomi means "pleasant one," and the Lord "has dealt very bitterly with me" (Ruth 1:20). But through the quiet, unobtrusive presence of a foreigner in Naomi's household, God opened the path to healing for the pain of the past, and brought joy for the present and hope for the future. For it was Ruth who found the "near kinsman" and brought the redemption of this ancient type of Christ to Naomi's door.

For Mephibosheth, there was David. Orphaned at the age of

5, physically handicapped, a fugitive in hiding from a king who sat on a throne that was rightfully his, Mephibosheth summed up his battle with shame in one despairing question for David: What do you want with such a dead dog as I am? (see 2 Sam. 9:8). But David's mind revisited a meadow with his dearest friend Jonathan. There, years before, he had entered into covenant to care for Jonathan's children should anything befall him. Through the magnanimous gestures of David, who restored to Mephibosheth all the lands owned by Saul and Jonathan, placed 37 personal servants at his disposal, and granted him a place at the king's own table as the king's own son, this representative of all humankind comes to understand the meaning of covenant and thus the God of everlasting covenant whom David represents.

For Solomon, there was Shulamith. To meet his need for assurance of his personal worth as a friend and companion that ran deeper than the acclaim showered on a king because of who he was and what he could give in exchange (S. of Sol. 1:6; 3:7, 8, 10), Shulamith offered much genuine affirmation and many gestures of love—for which she expected nothing in return (S. of Sol. 1:2-4, 13-14, 16; 2:3; 5:10-16; 7:11-13). If he desired intimacy and sexual fulfillment, she gave of herself unreservedly, moving their relationship steadily toward complete oneness of body, mind, and soul (S. of Sol. 2:4-6, 16-17; 4:16-5:1; 6:2-3; 7:6-9, 10-13; 8:11, 12, 14). When he sought the courage to face his innermost questions and fears, she continually invited his self-disclosure with her own (S. of Sol. 1:5-6, 7; 2:1; 3:1-4; 5:2-8). To fulfill his wish for total commitment, she extended her simple yet profound understanding of the marriage covenant— "My beloved is mine, and I am his" (S. of Sol. 2:16; 6:3; 7:10), her chastity and faithfulness (S. of Sol. 4:12; 8:10), and her utter confidence that despite conflict and disappointment, even wandering affections, it is possible under God for a man and a woman to find intimacy and to live out their lives under a banner of covenant love "as strong as death" (S. of Sol. 8:6, 7).

And for Shulamith, there was Solomon. Irrespective of her humble origin, the king took sheer delight in her simplicity and openness. If she saw herself a mere common lily of the field (S. of Sol. 2:1), Solomon declared her the most beautiful of them all (verse 2). Should she have any lingering doubts about her attractiveness (S. of Sol. 1:5, 6), Solomon showered her with superlatives about her beauty in his eyes (verse 15; 4:1-5; 6:4-10; 7:1-9). When she longed for tangible expressions of love, he showered her with gifts (S. of Sol. 7:11), affirmation (S. of Sol. 1:9; 4:7, 10), and terms of endearment (S. of Sol. 1:9, 15; 2:10, 14; 5:2; 6:9). The desire for closeness and companionship (S. of Sol. 1:7; 3:1-4; 5:4-8) brought invitations to springtime outings (S. of Sol. 2:10-14) and to an intimate rendezvous (verses 3, 6; 4:6-11). And if she yearned for covenant, there was fidelity (S. of Sol. 6:9), though sadly only for a time. But even in the midst of broken promises and unfaithfulness, there emerged an enduring poem that paints an exquisite portrait of God's design for marriage, rich in colors from the palate of wisdom mixed in the kaleidoscope of hindsight and what might have been.

But for all of us, there is the God-man, Jesus Christ, who is unlike any other. Everything comes together in Him. In heavenly places He reigns as Creator and Lord, and bestows worth upon all His creation by virtue of His eternal sovereignty and omnipotence. On earth He became "flesh and dwelt among us" (John 1:14). He came to earth to fulfill the demands of a holy law by dying the death which was ours that "in Him" we might have the abundant life which is His. Beyond that He demonstrated to us in ways that we could see and hear and touch the essence of divinity—agape love—and then taught us how to live under its banner.

From the beginning, the long, chilling shadow of the cross cast an ominous hue across His ministry. His birth in a cave amidst the animals of sacrifice, the wrappings of swaddling cloth, His name, the gifts of burial spices born by the Magi—all foreshadowed the relentless march of His life toward Calvary's hill. There, while the cosmos held its breath, He "bore our sins in His own body on the tree" (1 Peter 2:24). There He endured a yawning chasm between Himself and the Father. All that by His wounds we might be healed.

No one who ever lived was more goal-oriented, more unswerving in His purpose, than He. Always His eyes were locked on Calvary. Yet for all His relentless sense of mission, He never forgot the people who needed His healing touch, then and now, in practical, human ways they could feel. A leper. Ten lepers. Some pushy mothers and a caboodle of kids. A cripple on a stretcher lowered through the ceiling. Naked demoniacs bursting from tombs. A despairing woman who had merely touched the fringe of His cloak. A Samaritan floozie at the village well. A bantam-sized tax agent in a tree. A blind beggar sitting on the shoulder of the Jerusalem expressway. A friend who had just betrayed Him. A repentant felon on the cross next door. Always He found time and energy. Always He provided answers for the needs of the moment, but more significantly, for the deeper longings of the heart.

It is this same Jesus who anoints our eyes the second time so that we will see the men and women around us not as mere objects walking, but as "bruised reeds" and "smoking flax" (Matt. 12:20), who need both the good news of His atoning sacrifice and our shared encouragement to face life's battle. Jesus calls us by His perfect love to a higher plane of Christian living, to a love for one another uncharacteristic of fallen human beings and unattainable in our own strength (1 John 4:11). As surely as "He has borne our griefs and carried our sorrows" (Isa. 53:4), He motions us to "bear one another's burdens" (Gal. 6:2). And the healing that went out from His robe He invites us to carry personally to family, friends, and the world beyond.

Everywhere He went the lame walked, the blind saw, the mute sang, the discouraged found hope and new reasons for living. What practical means for binding up the brokenhearted might we learn from following His dusty footprints? Watch him as He reaches out to touch the pitiful remains of those ravaged by yesteryear's counterpart to AIDS. Listen as He comforts weary mothers and calms their restless children with His winsome smile and warm lap. See Him pause to offer hope to a woman who had nearly given up, acceptance to an outcast, forgiveness to a traitor, personal attention to countless forgettable little people with hungry hearts. Feel His look of grace penetrate the cocky facade of a loser. Bask in His unconditional love for innumerable victims trying to cope with life's darkness.[10]

Brenda Hunter in her book *Beyond Divorce* tells of the

excruciating anguish of infidelity, and the nearly unbearable feelings of rejection, loneliness, overload, and shame that came in the wake of her divorce. She relates how she would go to Howard Johnson's to eat, just so she could sit in a room full of happy people, hoping against hope that the waitress would act like she cared, maybe brush her arm as she passed.

Healing was a slow and painful process, which began only after she felt the encircling arms of a caring Christian community who took her in, bitter and resentful as she was, and offered her God's love "with skin on." Among these followers of Christ she found people who delighted in each other's company, sharing meals and projects of mutual interest, as well as one another's pain and concern about things like impoverished finances, problems with children, and important life decisions. In their company she found forgiveness and a new beginning.

Afterward she wrote, "I believe the church, when functioning properly, can provide healing for those who come. Within the church exists the necessary structure, the philosophical framework, and the power to deal with people and their problems. . . . But the church members must be willing to give up their isolation and total pursuit of material comfort in order to become involved in other people's lives." [11]

Earl Wilson in his book *A Silence to Be Broken*, which addresses the long road to healing for incest victims, isolates the factors essential to creating an atmosphere that will permit healing from shame, no matter what its cause, to take place. He concludes that such a healing atmosphere has five key components: a growing understanding of God's great love, openness and vulnerability, a strong awareness of the present impact of sin and shame, a heavy emphasis on grace, and nonjudgmental, noncritical input. [12] His list has given us cause for long pause as we have reflected on the atmosphere of our home, our church, our workplace, our community.

We once heard an old fable relating a contest between the seasons. Winter, Summer, Fall, and Spring were talking together. Spying a traveler walking along the road, Summer suggested to the others, "Behold yon traveler with his cloak upon him. Let us see which of us can persuade him to take it off."

They all accepted the challenge, each sure of victory.

Autumn went first. "I shall blow it away from him." The traveler felt his cloak billow in the wind and nearly lost it a time or two, but the harder the wind gusted, the tighter he gathered his coat about him, clinging to it as if for dear life.

Winter went next: "I will freeze the coat and make it so stiff that it will be unbearable." As the coat became heavier and heavier from snow and sleet, the traveler's neck began to chafe, and it became harder and harder to walk. But the traveler thought, *Difficult as it is, I must hang on to my coat, for at least it protects me from the elements.*

Spring tried next: "I will soak the coat. Then it will become so soggy and heavy, surely the traveler will discard it." So Spring rained and rained, until the coat became a great weight upon the traveler's shoulders, slowing his pace to a near standstill. But still the traveler wore his coat, reasoning he was better off with it than without it, and even if he removed it, he would have to carry it anyway.

Finally it came Summer's turn. The sun simply shone until the warmth of its rays penetrated the cloak and lured the traveler out from under his wraps into the pleasant sunshine. And the traveler smiled as he packed away his coat in an old trunk of things he didn't need anymore.

It's a fable, to be sure. But like most fables, it conveys more than a little truth.

---

[1] William Irvine and Park Honan, *The Book, the Ring, and the Poet* (New York: McGraw-Hill Books Co., 1974), p. 150.

[2] Elvan Kintner, ed., *The Letters of Robert Browning and Elizabeth Barrett Browning, 1845-1846* (The Belknap Press of Harvard University Press: Cambridge, Mass., 1969), Vol. I, p. 65 (May 15, 1845), quoted in Irvine and Honan, p. 150.

[3] *Ibid.*, p. 265 (Nov. 12, 1845), quoted in Irvine and Honan, p. 179.

[4] *Ibid.*, p. 261 (Nov. 9, 1845), quoted in Irvine and Honan, p. 179.

[5] *Ibid.*, p. 514 (Mar. 3, 1846), quoted in Irvine and Honan, p. 195.

[6] *Ibid.*, Vol. II, p. 836 (July 2, 1846), quoted in Irvine and Honan, p. 199.

[7] *Ibid.*, Vol. I, p. 324 (Dec. 18, 1845), quoted in Irvine and Honan, p. 189.

[8] *Ibid.*, Vol. II, p. 927 (Aug. 3, 1846), quoted in Irvine and Honan, p. 207.

[9] Irvine and Honan, p. 201.

[10] Selected imagery and ideas for the previous four paragraphs used by permission from Larry Libby, "The Corner of His Eye," *Discipleship Journal* (1990): 16-18.

[11] Brenda Hunter, *Beyond Divorce* (Old Tappan: N. J.: Fleming H. Revell, 1978), p. 56.

[12] Earl Wilson, *A Silence to Be Broken* (Portland, Oreg.: Multnomah Press, 1986), p. 118.

CHAPTER 7

Relationships to Cheer About

S everal years ago now we discovered a poem in *Moody Monthly* that instantly became a favorite. Its author, Mark Littleton, who, it turns out, lives only a few miles from us, has kindly consented to our sharing it with you.

When God made light, the angels
drew near to let the refractions roll
over their faces like a symphony.

When God made earth, they poked
their fingers into its moistness;
they put a fleck to their nose
and smiled.

When God made the sea, they kicked
at the foam and sat in its cool
till their bones laughed.

When God made a rose, they parted
its petals and passed it among
themselves, saying, "So fragile,
yet how it grasps the soul."

When God made a giraffe,

they touched the strange hide
and murmured to themselves that God
was up to something magnificent.

When God made man, each one
retired to his chamber and peered
into the writings, looking for some
clue to the mystery.

When God made woman, they came
back out of their chambers and gazed,
their jaws slack with awe.

When God joined man to woman
and said, "Let them become one flesh,"
everything suddenly made sense.
The cheering still shakes
the galaxies.[1]

Who's Around Your Trampoline?

Our Creator made human beings for relationships. He is a personal being who seeks fellowship with His creation, and He implanted a desire for companionship at the core of our being as well. It is one of the great paradoxes of our age that on a planet growing ever more densely populated and crowded, so many feel lonely and isolated. Many long for a nurturing circle of family and friends and a God who cares.

Donald Joy, in his book *Bonding: Relationships in the Image of God*, illustrates our need for human relationships by picturing people as having an inner relational "trampoline," held taut on each of its four sides by one's immediate family, extended family, friends, and close work associates.[2] To be emotionally and relationally healthy, to have "bounce" in our lives, Joy reports we need five to eight people supporting each side of our "trampoline."

Such individuals are not distant relatives, mere acquaintances, or friends of long ago with whom we may exchange a holiday greeting or a passing nod. To be part of the supporting network of relationships crucial to healthy living, they must be people with whom we are in frequent contact, people we would go out of our way to encounter, people for whom we would gladly drop what we are doing for the pleasure of a few minutes of talk. The overall tenor of such relationships are positive, affirmation runs freely, and we feel a lingering sense of celebra- tion that we have found each other. These kinds of relationships have within them assurance that no matter what trouble might befall either of us, the other would willingly make personal sacrifices to help, and nobody would think of keeping score. The Song of Songs offers insights into how to form and maintain such relationships both within friendship and in the special intimacy of marriage.

Let's Investigate the Mysteries of Bonding

The scriptural term for the process of human bonding is "cleave," a Hebrew verb meaning "to be joined together," "to adhere," "to stick." The book of Job uses the verb to speak of rows of scales on a sea creature: "One is so near another that no air can come between them; they are joined one to another, they stick together and cannot be parted" (Job 41:16, 17). The word describes how, after a long battle with the Philistines, the hand of David's warrior literally "stuck" to his sword (2 Sam. 23:10). And it characterizes the Psalmist's devotion to the testimonies of the Lord (Ps. 119:31). Daniel applied the term in the opposite sense, noting how impossible it is for iron to cleave to clay (Dan. 2:43). The Bible employs the same word for relationships between human beings and God (Deut. 10:20), between friends (Prov. 18:24), and within the covenant of marriage (Gen. 2:24).

In *The Ministry of Healing* Ellen White observed that all parts of the human organism, including "the senses, the faculties of the mind, . . . were placed under law." [3]   We are accustomed to thinking of the laws of health and the laws that govern the physical development of human beings from babyhood into adulthood. But we do not so often consider how God also placed human senses and emotions under divine law. The Creator not only gave us as human beings the desire to be in relationship with others, but He inscribed within us a script—something like a computer program or pattern—for bonding. Though marred by sin, its remnants remain written on every heart. It is a piece of the image of our Maker permanently imprinted on the human soul.

That script directs our total person in relationship to others. Since the Bible consistently sees humankind wholistically, it is not surprising that Scripture presents bonding as a wholistic process involving the entire being. It fully incorporates all of the physical senses as well as the emotions and the intellect. Stories of friends and lovers from Genesis to Revelation all depict this process, and the Song of Songs richly displays the fundamental elements of human bonding.

Both friendship and the bonding that will eventually lead to the "one flesh" intimacy of marriage follow a common pathway in the beginning. But in God's plan there comes a fork in the path where the bonding for friendship alone and that of marriage partners take different courses. However, both are wholistic experiences with physical, emotional, mental, and spiritual aspects.

The Senses and the Song

The development of the relationship between Solomon and Shulamith in the Song of Songs reveals the integral role played by the five senses in the bonding process:

You have ravished my heart, . . .
With one *look* of your eyes (S. of Sol. 4:9).

O my dove, in the clefts of the rock, . . .
Let me *see* your countenance,
Let me *hear* your voice;
For your voice is sweet,
And your countenance is lovely (S. of Sol. 2:14).

While the king is at his table,
My spikenard sends forth its *fragrance*.
A bundle of myrrh is my beloved to me,
That lies all night between my breasts (S. of Sol. 1:12, 13).

Like an apple tree among the trees of the woods,
So is my beloved among the sons.
I sat down in his shade with great delight,
And his fruit was *sweet* to my *taste* (S. of Sol. 2:3).

Your lips, O my spouse,
Drip as the honeycomb;
Honey and milk are under your *tongue*;
And the *fragrance* of your garments
Is like the fragrance of Lebanon (S. of Sol. 4:11).

His left hand is under my head,
And his right hand *embraces* me (S. of Sol. 2:6).

Problems always arise when we try to fragment human beings into component parts, however, and we must realize that the physical senses form but a part of a complex interaction. Taste, touch, hearing, sight, and smell are but the external sensors that trigger the formation of the emotional, mental, and spiritual ties. The Song reveals the development of ever-deepening bonds of friendship, love, and covenant:

Tell me, O you whom I love,
Where you feed your flock,
Where you make it rest at noon.
For why should I be as one who veils herself
By the flocks of your companions? (S. of Sol. 1:7).

This is my beloved,
And this is my friend (S. of Sol. 5:16).

My dove, my perfect one,
Is the only one (S. of Sol. 6:9).

My beloved is mine, and I am his.
He feeds his flock among the lilies (S. of Sol. 2:16).

Set me as a seal upon your heart,
As a seal upon your arm;
For love is as strong as death (S. of Sol. 8:6).

A Progressive Bonding Sequence

We are indebted again to Donald Joy, who introduced us to the steps in human pair-bonding. Joy compares with Scripture the observations of a biologist and anthropologist who has studied the process of human bonding across several cultures.[4] These observations bring from the natural world pieces of the puzzle that complement those provided by God's written revelation, giving us a more complete picture of God's design. Because outward manifestations of a deepening bond are more readily observable, the physical evidences that accompany the emotional, intellectual and spiritual levels of bonding mark the transition points to deeper and deeper attachment.

Perhaps a few anecdotes from the development of our own bond will serve to illustrate the process which has been observed to be universal in its basic components.

Ron: I remember vividly the first time I saw Karen. I was sitting in a row with my friends from the theology crowd at the midday prayer meeting my second year in college. In came a gaggle of girls, with one short one in their midst, laughing and talking and covered with freckles. I could not remember ever seeing her before, but my heart went "Ah-ha!" It did a second "Ah-ha!" minutes later when she volunteered to play the piano. She needed no music, and as her fingers ran up and down the keys, my mind wandered ahead to all those prayer meetings and evangelistic meetings when it would be so nice to have a built-in pianist . . . but how to proceed? We had no mutual friends. Coming as I did from the farm, more of my female acquaintances had been cows than girls, so I was not that skilled in starting a relationship. But I knew I *must* meet this girl.

In the first step of the bonding process, one sees the other, arousing interest in learning more about him or her.

Karen: I knew who Ron Flowers was because he led our prayer band sometimes. My friends and I affectionately called him Farmer Flowers because we thought he wore his pants too long. But it wasn't until we were among the few students left on campus during a short break that I remember our first significant encounter. I had wandered with a girlfriend to the student center on Saturday night, hoping to find somebody else with whom to while away the evening. We found only two—Ron and another theology major looking for the same thing. The four of us played games, sang around the piano, and talked until the student center closed and the two guys walked us back to the dorm. It was snowing softly, I remember. I mused to my friend as we slipped into our bunks, "You know, that Ron Flowers is really quite nice."

In order for the process of relationship formation to continue, the look of interest must be returned.

Ron: We know we will certainly date ourselves, but ours was the era when telephones first appeared in Adventist college dorm rooms—legally. What a boon they were to budding relationships! My roommate and I worked out a fairly equitable schedule, and oh, how I looked forward to talking with Karen. There was just something about the sound of her voice. You know what I'm talking about. Even as you read, you aren't that interested in our story, for it evokes memories of your own. Ours is the story of a bond that progressed through to the marriage covenant. You may be thinking of a bond with a friend.

The voice plays an ever-deepening role in the process of human bonding, for bonds cannot exist without communication.

Karen: Human touch also plays an important role, both for friends and for lovers. The formation of a lasting bond elicits ever-deepening levels of touch appropriate—within God's design—to the kind and the stage of the relationship and to the level of commitment and covenant made to one another.

I remember well the first time Ron took my hand. It had its amusing setting, under the table with the girls' dean standing less than a foot away, dressed as a snowman for the college Christmas party. But it was a highly significant landmark in our developing relationship. *Human beings reserve warm touch for those we genuinely care for.*

Ron: The time had come for the world to know. I had plans for this friendship. *At this level the encircling gesture of the arm placed around the shoulder signals to all who might be interested that the relationship is going somewhere.*

Karen: I worry a bit about myself when I think of this part of the story because the incident to this day brings me altogether too much glee! It was winter break, and a large group of us had planned to go on a three-day canoe trip. We were properly chaperoned, and had made careful plans to explore yet another river in the northern regions of Michigan. A girl whose name I have not forgotten (though many others are lost to memory) invited herself on the trip. I was convinced that she wished that she had been Ron's companion. Imagine my inner delight when within the first five minutes on the river, she stood up in her canoe. I may not be the world's best sportswoman, but I do know you don't stand up in a canoe. My ecstasy knew no bounds when in a matter of seconds she dumped herself, her partner, and all the canoe's contents into the mucky but shallow river. It was beside the fire we had to build to get her dried out that the significant event occurred. As we stood there warming ourselves, Ron put his arm around my shoulder. And I thought to myself, *Carole my dear [not her real name], I hope you notice and that the message is clear!*

Ron: By this time the fork in the bonding pathway between friendship bonding and pair-bonding has taken place. Deepening levels of physical intimacy, inappropriate for "just friends" and persons of the same sex, will now occur in pair-bonding. Emotional, intellectual, and spiritual ties, however, continue to deepen as both pathways extend. *For couples, the next relational level involves a growing investment in the relationship. It is a time when dreams and goals and hopes for the future occupy many hours of sharing.* "What ifs" of a future together play over and over in the mind. Karen and I didn't have much money, so we walked, arm in arm, for hours during this period. I remember asking her out of the blue, "Would you ever go with me to India?" Little did I dream our ministry together would one day actually take us there. We weren't ready to talk seriously of marriage yet, but we were just thinking ahead.

Karen: It was time to talk of more than dreams and school-work and life on campus. *Observations of couples in various cultures have highlighted a significant outward change marking the entrance of deepening levels of communication in a relationship.* The two who had been facing the world side by side as they dreamed, now turned face to face, and intense self-disclosure began. For this level of communication to have come any earlier would have been unthinkable—we were not ready to take the risk. But now we began to share deeper, more personal feelings and thoughts. The other day I was digging through the attic for something and came across an old box of love letters. I must admit they were a disappointment. Now, after 26 years of sharing so deeply, they seemed shallow and frivolous. But at the time they represented the biggest risk we could take.

The next stages in the process of human bonding represent deepening levels of trust. Joy notes that when two people allow each other to touch their heads, it indicates unconditional acceptance. But at the same time we both become more and more vulnerable to each other and more and more comfortable with revealing who we really are inside. We open up to each other because we see growing evidence that there is safety from shame and betrayal. It is a time when, despite the full awareness that the loved one is not perfect, we experience acceptance and love.

The final stages in pair-bonding the Bible terms "one flesh." God in His wisdom always places these bonding steps within the framework of the marriage covenant. The physical acts of love represent the total giving of oneself to a married partner—spiritually, emotionally, and mentally—in the most personal, intimate expression of love that God has enabled us to show.

Glimpsing the Bonding Sequence in the Song

While the Song introduces all the basic elements of human bonding, the nonchronological sequence of the various scenes tends to obscure the complete sequence of phenomena that accompany the various levels of a developing bond. Song of Solomon 2:8-17 comes the closest to showing all of it. This passage sweeps the reader grandly from an early courtship experience, when the king invites his mountain darling to a springtime outing, into their married experience, when the wife invites her beloved husband to a time of intimacy with her.

Gazing upon each other, hearing each other's voice, spending enjoyable time together—all these build the relationship. They give each other affirmation and convey wishes as an invitation, not a command. Deep levels of personal disclosure take place. She expresses her feelings of acceptance of him through the contrast between the fox and the gazelle. A fox rampages among the tender grapevines, but her beloved is a gentle gazelle who "browses" (verse 16, NIV), taking emotional and physical delight in her. The miniature marriage formula, "My beloved is mine and I am his," proclaims their trust in each other, their vulnerability before each other.

What transpires throughout the development of a relationship of a man and a woman before marriage can provide a solid foundation for their commitment to each other in the marriage itself. Bonding that takes place slowly, allowing all the steps that God designed we should experience, that focuses, in the latter half of the sequence at least, on one exclusive partner, and reaches the final stages at a time when both partners are emotionally mature—that bonding, we believe, stands the best chance of continuing happiness.

Sure bonding, lasting intimacy. There is romance here, and there is mystery. And that is something to cheer about!

---

[1] Mark Littleton, "Marriage," *Moody Monthly*, February 1987.

[2] Donald Joy, *Bonding: Relationships in the Image of God* (Waco, Tex.: Word, 1985), p. 4.

[3] Ellen G. White, *The Ministry of Healing* (Mountain View, Calif.: Pacific Press, 1942), p. 415.

[4] Donald Joy, *Bonding: Relationships in the Image of God*, pp. 41-53.

CHAPTER 8

Return to Eden

Recently some young friends of ours gave us the great honor of participating in their wedding ceremony. Eight months earlier Bobby and Jackie had come to us, enjoying a good friendship, attracted to each other, musing about marriage, but genuinely wondering whether it would be a wise idea. Imagine our delight when, after several appointments, they announced their engagement. That delight doubled when they invited us both to have a part in their wedding service.

It was a day for making memories. Enraptured by the setting, the music, the inspiring words of the minister, and most of all the presence of his beautiful bride, the groom excitedly replied to the question "Will you take this woman . . . ?" with a resounding "I sure will!" His romantic flair overcame all inhibitions when, upon their introduction as husband and wife, he boldly scooped her into his arms and strode exuberantly off the rostrum down several steep steps to the sanctuary floor.

The joy and excitement of sharing in the wedding of our friends lingers with us as we work on this chapter focusing on marriage in the Song of Songs. Rapture and delight also marked the wedding of Solomon and Shulamith. The poem refers to the occasion in superlative tones as "the day of the gladness of his heart" (S. of Sol. 3:11). The Song preserves several brief glimpses of the festivities. The first dramatizes the procession of the portable royal carriage with its impressive military escort bearing Solomon and his bride. Then the forward action freezes as the queen mother bestows the wedding coronet on her son (verses 6-11). Song of Solomon 6:11-13, on the other side of the chiasm, features Shulamith. The verses here are a little obscure, but apparently tell of her departure from her mountain home in the midst of escorting chariots, and then her performance of a ceremonial wedding dance (''turn'' or ''return'' has the sense of ''whirl'') before the two assembled groups, the members of the royal procession and the Jerusalem wedding party.

Even as a marriage is more than a ceremony, so the Song of Songs reveals more of God's design for the husband-wife relationship than it does the details of the wedding. It is a book about married love and intimacy, and both in and between the lines it presents a message about the wider aspects of sexuality as well, the celebration of our maleness and femaleness and of God's design for the relationship of the two genders of human-kind to each other. A message unique for its time, it especially speaks to us today. To bring its lessons into clearer perspective, we will look first at marriage and male-female relationships throughout history.

The Creation of Marriage

The Book of Beginnings (Gen. 1:26-28; 2:18-25) preserves two accounts of the creation of human beings. The first is a general record of the events of the sixth creation day, revealing that man and woman, male and female, are each the handiwork of the Creator. The account designates both as bearers of the ''image of God,'' states that both have dominion as coregents over creatures of land, sea, and sky, and that both share God's blessing and the responsibility for procreation. A most interesting Hebrew sentence construction occurs in Genesis 1:26, 27. It uses the singular word ''adam'' twice, not as the name of one of them, but as a designation for the human pair: ''Let us make *man* [*adam*] in Our image, after Our likeness; let *them* have dominion. . . . So God created *man* [*adam*] in His own image; in the image of God He created him; male and female He created *them*'' (verses 26, 27). Among other things, this unique construction reflects the unity and mutuality in marriage that God intended.

The complementary narrative in Genesis 2 shows us the actual processes whereby the man and woman came to be. This second account further emphasizes their relationship and illuminates how the intimate bond of marriage satisfies human need. The Creator declares, "It is not good that man should be alone; I will make him a helper comparable to him" (verse 18). "Helper" (Hebrew *ezer*) means "help" or "succor." Most of its Old Testament uses portray God helping, supporting, or providing physical, emotional, and spiritual sustenance in one way or another (cf. Deut 33:7, 26, 29; Ps. 70:5; 121:1, 2). The helper in Genesis 2 will be one who is suited to her husband, one with whom he can share mutual love, care, and understanding. She will "help" in a human way as God "helps" in a divine way. Helper, notes Old Testament scholar Richard Davidson, "is a relational term, describing a beneficial relationship, but in itself does not specify position or rank, either superiority or inferiority." [1]

Adam slept while God created the woman. Because a rib from his side supplied the substance from which God fashioned her, the two parts of humanity have a common origin, the same earthy raw material (cf. Gen. 2:7; 3:19). One is not superior to the other. Eden knows no competition, no disharmony, no inequality. The creation from the rib makes a symbolic statement. Writes Ellen White, echoing an old rabbinical tradition, "Eve was created from a rib taken from the side of Adam, signifying that she was not to control him as the head, nor to be trampled under his feet as an inferior, but to stand by his side as an equal, to be loved and protected by him." [2]

With poetic ecstasy the man receives the woman. Until this point, Genesis 2 has used *adam* to designate the person who awaits his companion. With her arrival, the special sexual distinctiveness of the two genders of humankind becomes evident. Scripture now calls "man" *ish* and the "woman" *ishshah*. They are two beings, yet complementary, harmonious parts of one humanity. Genesis 5:2 again indicates that so complete was their oneness "in the day they were created" that they had one name—"Adam" given them by God. Only after the account of the Fall do we read of the woman receiving the name "Eve."

At the end of Genesis 2 are the words establishing marriage as an institution. They link God's ideal for this covenant relationship clearly with the relationship of man and woman described at the time of their creation: "Therefore a man shall leave his father and mother and be joined to his wife, and they shall become one flesh" (Gen. 2:24).

Marriage After the Fall

When sin altered human nature at the Fall, the husband-wife relationship changed. The curse of sin affected the marriage relationship (Gen. 3:16). Henceforth, where sin reigned, marriage would suffer from selfishness, the quest for personal gratification, and the tendency to exploit or dominate another. In their sinless state neither of the sexes ruled the other. But now sin distorted their masculinity and femininity and adversely affected their delicate alignment in marriage.

The man dealt with the new situation by seizing supremacy, seeking to control his world around him. He approached all his relationships, including marriage, from this mind-set. Even his response to God immediately after the Fall displayed an air of arrogance and superiority (verse 12). Sin also tainted those unique feminine qualities and maternal instincts that God had given the woman. Now she would know pain in childbearing and a fervent desire (Hebrew *tesuqah*), a deep, perhaps inordinate, hunger for bonds of attachment in order to give life meaning.

No one loved the first pair more than God. No one longed to turn the clock back more than He. Graciously, He immediately set in motion a rescue operation whereby the couple might be forgiven, enabled by grace to continue their communion with God, and, in the fullness of redemptive time, be restored to Eden. Even in the midst of His delineation of the curses to come in the wake of sin, God proclaimed the good news of redemption from sin and its curse. A Saviour had been waiting in the wings since the foundation of the world—waiting in the person of their Creator and Friend. And the Seed of the woman would bruise the serpent's head (verse 15).

God's salvation effort did not immediately stay the tide of sin's consequences. Rather, Providence worked in and through the deplorable situation in which the first husband and wife found themselves to help contain the disastrous effects of sin.

"When God created Eve, He designed that she should possess neither inferiority nor superiority to the man, but that in all things she should be his equal. . . . But after Eve's sin, as she was first in the transgression, the Lord told her that Adam should rule over her. She was to be in subjection to her husband, and this was a part of the curse." [3]

Throughout history the lot of women has often been very bitter and their lives burdensome. Catherine Kroeger cites Greek sources illustrating the pagan male view that women were not fit to associate with civilized people. Women, they contended, "had been made as a sneaky trick of the gods in order to compensate for man having gained possession of fire." Created of substances inferior to those used to make man, this lesser order of being had neither the spiritual nor intellectual perceptions of man. The most virtuous woman, the Greek concept declared, was crass in comparison to the basest male. [4]

Even among God's professed followers, women fared but little better. Despite the ideals to which God continually called them by His precepts, the Hebrews often imitated their neighbors. The practices of taking more than one wife, of infidelity, and of easy divorce became commonplace. In the time of Christ, the Pharisees' daily devotional prayers included, "I thank God that I was not made a woman." Sadly, many in the Christian church have continued to heap shame upon women as well. Tertullian, an early Church Father, unleashed an astonishing tirade:

"You are the devil's gateway. You are the unsealer of the forbidden tree. You are the first deserter of the divine law. You are she who persuaded him [Adam] who the devil was not valiant enough to attack. You destroyed so easily God's image, man. As a dangerous seducer of men, let woman seclude herself, dress in sober garments, veil her face, and walk humbly in the earth." [5]

Many a woman even today can testify that the curse is alive and well. Around that curse has developed a model of marriage that even Christian circles perpetuate and defend. A popular Christian family seminar, which has drawn thousands for the past three decades, proclaims that the curse of Genesis 3 ("he shall rule over you") is *God's order for families.* Rather than proclaiming the redemptive gospel of Jesus, it embodies all the pagan wisdom of an ancient Persian court:

" 'If it please your majesty, let a royal decree go out from you and let it be inscribed in the laws of the Persians and Medes, never to be revoked, that Vashti shall not again appear before King Ahasuerus; and . . . Thus when this royal edict is heard through the length and breadth of the kingdom, all women will give honour to their husbands, high and low alike.' . . . Letters were sent to all the royal provinces, to every province in its own script and to every people in their own language, in order that each man might be master in his own house and control all his own womenfolk" (Esther 1:19-22, NEB).

The Redemption of Marriage

Praise God, the curse is not the gospel. Sin has perverted marriage, but the gospel seeks to restore its purity and beauty. Though the Saviour would come in the fullness of time to accomplish in fact what until then God's people could only accept by faith, bright shafts of redemptive light pierced through the cracks in the canopy of darkness that shrouded marriage even in old time. The prophets exalted marriage, using it to describe God's love, and they decried the abuses that befell the God-ordained relationship. All parts of the Hebrew Scriptures celebrated romance and friendship as well as covenant faithfulness between husband and wife—in the Law, the Prophets, and the Writings.

But if shadows prevailed before Christ, with Him the morning came. In Him the kingdom of God arrived. Though believers wait for full deliverance from sin until His second coming, by faith His followers find themselves rescued now from the powers of the present evil age and enabled to taste the powers of the age to come. In Him old things have passed away, all things are made new. As He dwells in human hearts by faith, His people may be "filled with all the fullness of God" (Eph. 3:19).

The New Testament insists that in Him believers can adopt new ways of relating to others that are as different from what is commonplace in society around them as light is from darkness.

Jesus Christ challenged the evils that had wedged their way between the sexes. Though He never married, He approved of marriage. That there could be no doubt, He took time on His march toward His destiny on Calvary to celebrate with a bride and groom. No couple ever received a greater wedding gift, for they were treated not only to His blessing, but to His first miracle. His supernatural transformation of water into wine at that wedding symbolized the passing away of an old, impoverished religious system and the arrival of a new, refreshing, vitalizing power in Christ. Later, in the most extravagant tribute thinkable, Jesus magnified marriage, making it a symbol of the union between Himself as the Bridegroom and the redeemed, His Bride. It is significant, too, that when our Lord addressed the subject of marriage directly, He supported His views from Genesis 1 and 2, not Genesis 3 (Matt. 19:4ff.). Christ did not assault the existing social structure of marriage directly, but presented viewpoints and perspectives that would alter human hearts and reshape marriage from the inside. In two specific ways He brought to light truth that confronted the curse that now governed the relationships between men and women.

One day two of His disciples schemed to manipulate their way to the highest levels of power in the government they expected Jesus to establish. James and John persuaded their mother to ask Him for seats on His right hand and on His left. Learning of the ploy, the other disciples grew indignant, probably because they hadn't thought of it first. Jesus, however, used the occasion to contrast sharply the way of the gospel with common practices in society. The rulers of the Gentiles lord it over their subjects, He pointed out, but "it shall not be so among you" (Matt. 20:26). Then the One who came not to be served but to serve heralded a seminal concept that would sound the death knell to all use of sinful power and control in relationships, that would overturn all hierarchical rulership—"Whoever wants to be great must be your servant, and whoever wants to be first must be the willing slave of all" (verse 26, NEB).

Christ also went about sensitively restoring the gender balance between the sexes. He began by lifting women from their inferior status. "Jesus treated women as *people*. He went out of His way to refute by His actions the attitudes toward women. . . . He insisted Mary of Bethany be allowed to sit at His feet and learn theology instead of being sent to the kitchen where custom would have placed her. He raised the woman taken in adultery to the human level of her accusers. The woman of Samaria was as surprised as His disciples that He would talk to her, a woman. But Jesus went further; He commissioned her to bring the Good News to her whole village."[6]

The renowned theologian John R. W. Stott saw the meaning in Christ's actions toward women: "Without any fuss or publicity, Jesus terminated the curse of the Fall, reinvested woman with her partially lost nobility, and reclaimed for his new kingdom community the original creation blessing of sexuality equality."[7]

The apostolic writers, too, were aware of entrenched social customs that shaped the lives of believers, customs that would change ever so slowly. Yet the apostles built on what Christ did. They boldly presented principles that contrasted with worldly practices, confident that Christian believers, under the guidance of the Spirit, would steadily grow into conformity to the will of God. Galatians 3:28 constitutes a Magna Carta for human relationships: "There is neither Jew nor Greek, there is neither slave nor free, there is neither male nor female; for you are all one in Christ Jesus." Faith in Christ abolishes all barriers, whether religious, cultural, or social, that separate people from each other. Discussing further the unity Christians know despite their background as Jews and Gentiles, Paul exalted the cross of Christ as the source of reconciliation. In doing so, he used language that one could as easily apply to the separation between male and female (Eph. 2:14-18). "To create out of the two a single new humanity in himself, thereby making peace" (NEB) is good news that addresses the curse on marriage in Genesis 3 and makes the way possible for couples to know the "one flesh" experience of Genesis 2.

The curse involved a subjection of the wife to the husband.

The gospel concept of mutual submission (Eph. 5:21) neutralizes the curse and its effects by emphasizing instead the love and service of husband and wife to each other. Paul inseparably links his instruction to wives to submit to their husbands as to the Lord (verse 22) with a command to husbands that both husbands and wives in the world of the first century must have received with astonishment: "Husbands, love your wives, just as Christ also loved the church and gave Himself for it" (verse 25). Peter also counsels wives to be submissive to their husbands, yet in the next breath he instructs husbands to apply their spiritual understanding to the marriage relationship and to bestow honor ("great worth") on their wives. Christ makes a difference in the marriage of Christians. A new mutuality prevails. Husbands and wives are "heirs together of the grace of life" (1 Peter 3:7).

Marriage in the Song of Songs

Such similarity exists between the man-woman relationship of Genesis 1 and 2 and that depicted in the Song of Solomon that a number of scholars have remarked that the Song is a "return to Eden." As a result, some think of it as an idyllic piece, a fantasy, rather than a serious description of a real relationship. The Song of Solomon evidences the "return to Eden" theme in several ways:

The titles given to the leading characters. "Shulamite" (S. of Sol. 6:13) and "Solomon" are male and female forms of the same Hebrew word. The two therefore share one name in a manner similar to the name "Adam" borne by the first couple (Gen. 1:27; 5:2).

Their friendship. Solomon and Shulamith have a relationship of genuine friendship. She calls him her friend (S. of Sol. 5:16) and his affectionate name for her, "my love," used over and over, means "my friend."

Individuality and freedom of choice. Repeatedly the pair extend invitations to each other. He invites her to a spring outing (S. of Sol. 2:10-13); she invites him to spend time with her (verse 17); he invites her to "come with me from Lebanon" (S. of Sol. 4:8); she invites him to enter her garden, which is "his garden" (verse 16). To invite is to recognize and respect the other's full personhood and freedom of choice.

Mutuality in marriage. "My beloved is mine and I am his" (S. of Sol. 2:16 and the reverse, S. of Sol. 6:3) is a miniature marriage covenant formula that succinctly expresses the sense of mutuality the couple knows. One does not control or have power over the other. Each freely gives himself to the other in marriage. "I am my beloved's, and his desire (Heb. *tesuqah*) is toward me" (S. of Sol. 7:10) restores the balance of desire distorted by the curse in Genesis 3:16.

The structure of the poem. The mirror-imaging of the chiasm, with its point and counterpoint and its two complementary parts making the whole, provides a literary device that corresponds to the equality and mutuality of the leading figures in their relationship. Specific segments on either side of the chiastic center balance each other.

Far from being fantasy, these qualities of the Song anticipate the redemption of male-female relationships that Christ accomplished and the New Testament unveils more fully. Here, offered to all by Solomon late in life as a final effort toward that which God had prepared him to do, was a preview of Christ's restoration of marriage to its original sanctity and elevated state.

Living by Faith the Life of Eden

Doubtless the principles for husband-wife relationships as redeemed by Christ and heralded in the Song of Songs run counter to those with which most of us have grown up. We shall each have to decide how to position ourselves between society's notions of leadership and family management on the one hand, ingrained as they are in religion, and the call of the gospel to equality, coregency, and mutuality on the other. In a discussion about the confrontation between Christ and culture we had with several African pastors, one put it this way: "I have joined a new tribe where Jesus is chief. I have a new set of tribal customs."

The power of God is mighty to save us and to change us. In *Fulton's Footprints in Fiji* Eric B. Hare tells of the conversion of Ratu Ambrose. The cruel chief had squandered the lives of many of his faithful subjects while pursuing his aggressive goals. Scarred and broken in body, one old fisherman, Matui, had survived the torturous experience of being one of the human "logs," men bound with ropes and used as rollers upon which Ratu Ambrose had launched his heavy war canoes.

Pastor John Fulton's evangelistic efforts brought both Ratu Ambrose and Matui into the same Seventh-day Adventist church. God's power to transform hearts and habits powerfully demonstrated itself when the new believers celebrated their first Lord's Supper and footwashing service. Ratu Ambrose quickly took a towel and basin and knelt down before Matui to wash his feet. The bent, elderly fisherman at first resisted. "It is not right for you to wash my feet; you are a great chief." As Ratu Ambrose went on to bathe the feet of his former subject with tears filling his eyes and his heart, he replied, "There is only one Chief here in this room tonight, and that is Jesus."

---

[1] Richard M. Davidson, "The Theology of Sexuality in the Beginning: Genesis 1-2," *Andrews University Seminary Studies*, 26 (No. 1): 15.

[2] Ellen G. White, *Patriarchs and Prophets* (Mountain View, Calif.: Pacific Press, 1958), p. 46.

[3] _____ , *Testimonies for the Church* (Mountain View, Calif.: Pacific Press, 1948), Vol. 3, p. 484.

[4] Gretchen Gaebelein Hull, *Equal to Serve* (Old Tappan, N.J.: Fleming H. Revell, 1969), pp. 277, 278.

[5] Alberta Mazat, *That Friday in Eden* (Mountain View, Calif.: Pacific Press, 1981), p. 29.

[6] Patricia Gundry, *Heirs Together* (Grand Rapids: Zondervan Pub. House, 1980), p. 46.

[7] John Stott, *Involvement: Social and Sexual Relationships in the Modern World* (Old Tappan, N.J.: Fleming H. Revell Co., 1984), p. 136.

CHAPTER 9

Lessons From
a Loving Couple

The pleasantly pungent scent and smoke of incense drifts toward the sky, mingling with the dust churned up along the crowded processional route. The royal carriage porters, their muscles straining, march with even cadence while on their shoulders they bear their regal cargo. An elite armed escort, 60 men strong, clears the way ahead and guards the flanks and rear. Praises and hosannas fill the air as eager spectators stretch on tiptoe to see His Majesty King Solomon and to glimpse the shy, deeply tanned Lebanese bride beside him. At the appointed wedding site, all the eyes of Jerusalem rest upon the youthful couple as they make their marriage vows to each other. Unlike his many political marriages that would later tear apart his own moral fabric as well as that of his nation, this wedding is a cause for rejoicing. The queen mother waits to crown her son with the wedding coronet and give her blessing to him and his bride. Through the brief autobiographical glimpse Solomon presents in Song of Solomon 3:6-11, we too can view the festivities.

The public ceremony ended, the scene shifts. The newlyweds retire to their private chamber. To our surprise, even astonishment, the Song of Songs opens this room to us as well. The word pictures of Song of Solomon 4:1-5:1 contain the most tender and sublime scenes of human marriage that God has given in His Word—the rapture a couple find in each other.

As we realized that we were being permitted to overhear the pillow talk of a couple on their wedding night, we experienced a flood of feelings. First came disbelief at what we were reading in the Bible. Then came the joy of discovering that God has not left out this part of human experience from His Word. We were curious to read on, yet uneasy. What right did we have to be here? Was this not a most private time and place?

I recall vividly our own concerns for privacy on our wedding night. Several of my college classmates had boasted that they knew the hotel where we had made reservations and planned to pay Karen and me a visit. Not knowing for sure what they knew or what prank they might be up to, we took no chances. When we left our wedding reception on the university campus where we were both students, we asked a friend in campus security to seal off the parking lot with his cruiser for a little while so that no one could follow us. While the blue lights of the campus police car guarded the exit behind us, we sped away with a trusted faculty member who chauffeured us to our secluded car. Safe thus far, we decided on one more precaution and stopped at a pay phone en route to our hotel just long enough to cancel our reservations and book a room in another hotel 30 miles further down the road. Even then, I remember being nervous, fully expecting my crafty companions to discover our whereabouts.

But the Song of Songs reveals no such nervousness. Of course, in reading the Song, we are not, as it were, bursting in like pranksters upon the couple's intimacy. God would never sanction such intrusion. But that we may behold the exquisite design of married love as it came from the hand of the Creator, the couple and yes, God Himself (who has preserved this piece of biblical literature over long centuries for us) invite us to read on. Our heavenly Father has something wonderful in store for us.

A Discomforting Contrast

The openness and candor with which the Song addresses the intimate acts of married love may make us uncomfortable because the Song apparently disregards two commonly held convictions.

The intermarital taboo. First, it seemingly ignores a universal unwritten rule passed down from generation to generation that married couples do not disclose their marital experience to others. One culture will soundly beat a wife who shares the intimate details of her marriage with another. In a myriad of other corners of the earth we have sensed the awkwardness people have in finding words to ask about sexuality. The anxiety that grips couples who sense their need for help in their marriages may take days, weeks, even years to overcome.

This unwritten rule about marital disclosure, sometimes called the "intermarital taboo," represents both a piece of God's intent and a tragic distortion. When it represents a sacred circle that gives a family identity, security, and appropriate privacy, it is helpful. But it is harmful when it creates a wall of seclusion that traps spouses or children in hurtful relationships that could benefit from learning new relational skills. It is devastatingly destructive when it cloaks abuse. And it is sadly isolating when it deprives us all of a much-needed wider circle of companionship and support. We can testify that some of the moments in which our marriage has grown the most have occurred in the presence of other couples who felt the freedom to share the workings of God in their married lives so that others might find the courage to pursue their own journey toward oneness.

Sex and spirituality don't mix. The sexually explicit themes of the Song go against yet another deeply ingrained conviction—that sex and spirituality are incompatible. While sexual intercourse for procreation is obviously a necessity, many suffer from a lingering worry that sexual pleasure between husbands and wives may violate a thoroughgoing holiness. Once we read to a marriage enrichment group one of our favorite quotations about the holiness of physical married love. "Angels of God will be guests in the home, and their holy vigils will hallow the marriage chamber." [1] One wife across the circle immediately became visibly agitated. Cupping her hand to her mouth, she exclaimed, "Oh, no!" Little did we imagine the pain that hid behind her gesture. Privately the couple later shared with us their agony. At

the heart of their struggle lay voices from her childhood. Sex, her
background had drilled into her, was only for having babies. And
really good Christians must put away sexual activity in preparation for translation. Imagine her distress when she thought she
heard us saying that angels were checking up on her!

This contrast between the Song and what is socially and
religiously acceptable has disturbed religious people as far back
as we have record. Over the centuries they have viewed the Song
as a source of embarrassment, religious confusion, even heresy.
Church prelates have regularly condemned, even destroyed the
writings of those who insisted upon its literal, natural interpretation. Shrill voices have called for religious leaders to throw the
book out of the Sacred Canon. Sadly, for much of Christian
history, the church has tolerated the beautiful love poem only
because of the allegorical interpretation given its lines. Through
the allegorization of its every phrase and symbol it has transformed the Song from "an hot carnall pamphlet," as the English
Westminster Assembly put it, to an expression of spiritual love
without fleshly taint.

Some religious teachers have rightly sensed that part of the
difficulty raised by the Song lies within the readers themselves.
But their solutions only put further distance between the book and
the people. One had to "qualify" in order to study the Song. The
Hebrew sages allowed only those 25 years of age and older to
read it. Origen, in keeping with the Greek philosophy of dualism
that colored his thinking, kept it out of reach of everyone "who
is not yet rid of the vexations of flesh and blood and has not
ceased to feel the passion of his bodily nature." [2] Jerome (c.
340-420) counseled that one should thoroughly study every other
Bible book and memorize most of the Old Testament before one
could safely read the Song of Songs! Yet through it all God has
had His hand over the Song and its message for relationships in
all times.

Called to Be "Naked and Unashamed"
The openness and candid portrayal of sexuality in the Song
testify to the gap that exists between marriage today and the
Edenic blueprint when "they were both naked, the man and his

wife, and were not ashamed" (Gen. 2:25). In Eden the first couple did not have to resort to hiding or secretiveness when discussing their sexuality. No awkwardness or rift existed between sexuality and spirituality. Listen as Old Testament authority E. J. Young describes the role the book plays:

"The Song . . . is didactic and moral in its purpose. It comes to us in this world of sin, where lust and passion are on every hand, where fierce temptations assail us and try to turn us aside from the God-given standard of marriage. And it reminds us, in particularly beautiful fashion, how pure and noble true love is. . . . By its very inclusion in the Canon, it reminds us of a love that is purer than our own." [3]

The apostle Paul observes, "I would not have known sin except through the law" (Rom. 7:7). The sharp contrast the law reveals between God's standard and our condition prods us to an awareness of our need. So also with the Song. We must not alter the Song's message to suit us, but *we* must let the Spirit transform us into its ideals. The Song of Solomon beckons us toward the Edenic experience of being "naked and unashamed." Certainly, if we are to believe the rest of the Bible, it is not an excited state reserved only for the passions of young love, nor is it safely opened only to relationships whose passions religious propriety have subdued. Rather it is an intimacy and oneness that lies at the heart of the Creator's design. Nothing but God's grace can prepare us for the Song and can work that change in us that will bring us closer to its ideals. For only God's love made our own can turn marriage into the dynamic, ever-opening, ever-accepting, ever-discovering, ever-deepening relationship portrayed in the Song of Songs.

Winsome Words: Our Terms of Endearment

Perhaps with a bit more comfort now we may return to the bridal chamber. In its intimate setting we hear Solomon and Shulamith whispering their affirmations, their affectionate names for each other. "Behold, you are fair, my love [*rayahti*]!" he cries with delight as he looks at her. Later she invites him, "Let my beloved [*dodi*] come to his garden." Names say a lot about the kind of closeness a couple share and the emotional temperature of a relationship. *Rayahti* and *Dodi* are cozy pet names that enfold and warm the heart, and at the same time delight and excite it.

How different from the names permitted in a home not far from where I grew up. There lived in our community a family I will call Jones. The iron-fisted father ruled his household as some medieval knight might have lorded it over his serfs. So rigid was he that he insisted his wife address him at all times as "Mr. Jones."

Now my wife has called me "Mr. Flowers" after I tracked mud in on the kitchen floor she had just scrubbed. But I much prefer "H. B." (for "Honey-bunches") and she is my "Babe." I have no idea how we started using the terms, and somehow on paper they seem a little silly, but we each wear them like well-worn slippers. They are uniquely ours, as I discovered one day when I phoned my wife's office. Fully expecting her to answer, I said exuberantly, "Hi, Babe," before the female voice on the other end of the line got out the words, "Church Ministries, this is Carlene. I am *not* Babe!" the voice further affirmed. It was our secretary!

Compliments, the emotional lifeblood of relationships, flow freely throughout the Song and are especially intimate in Song of Solomon 4:1-5:1. Comparisons to animals, precious stones, fruits, even buildings, help give voice to feelings and sensations. Mountains depict her charms. To him, her teeth are like shorn sheep, her hair like a flock of goats on a mountainside. We appreciated the comparison with goats more after a Lebanese pastor in one of our seminars pictured for us the black goats common to his homeland. As the herdsmen lead their huge flocks homeward in the evening, they stream like rivulets down the mountainside, their ebony coats glistening in the setting sun. The sense of many of Solomon's compliments escape the modern reader, and we may well have not understood them even then. However, Shulamith knew what he meant! This is love's language, encoded and decoded by the couple. All of these verses contain this kind of intimate, playful pillow talk that loving couples know.

Solomon's greatest compliment is a commentary on true love.

"You are all fair, my love, and there is no spot in you" (S. of Sol. 4:7). Every loved one will have flaws and imperfections, though young love tends not to detect them. Happy is the couple who, after the early intensity of romance abates, can still say of each other, "There is no flaw in you" (RSV). "Love will cover a multitude of sins," Peter explains (1 Peter 4:8). "There is no flaw in you" says as much about the lover as about the one loved. It speaks of the deep value the lover bestows upon the beloved. Truly it is a look born of heaven, seated in the love of the Father who declares, "You are my beloved child in whom I am well pleased," cloaking our imperfections in the seamless white robe of His only begotten Son.

Differences in Loving for Him and Her

Many verses in the poem highlight the well-documented fact that men and women tend to experience love in somewhat different ways. Men can quickly become aroused romantically through visual stimuli and by touching their mates. Note Solomon's many references to seeing her face (S. of Sol. 2:14), delighting in her physical beauty (S. of Sol. 4:1ff.; 6:4ff; 7:1ff), being captured by her hair (S. of Sol. 7:5), holding the "branches" (verse 8), and embracing her (S. of Sol. 2:6; 8:3). Women, on the other hand, respond more to the overall quality of the relationship. Emotional intimacy and the commitment of their husbands to them and their children rank high in their priorities. Romantically women respond best in an atmosphere that is unhurried, with time for plenty of words of love and affirmation accompanied by closeness and caressing. Shulamith links herself with women of all time by her references to her yearnings to be with him (S. of Sol. 1:7), her desires for his companionship and friendship (S. of Sol. 2:3, 10; 5:16; 7:11ff.), her fears of separation from him (S. of Sol. 3:1; 5:6), and her pleas for his committed love (S. of Sol. 8:6, 7). She enjoys having him kiss, hold, and caress her (S. of Sol. 1:2; 2:6; 8:3). The extended loving remarks of the husband (S. of Sol. 4:1-15) to which the wife responds (verse 15) highlight this difference in sexual response.

One Flesh: The Ultimate Return to Eden

The Song revolves around two delicately worded verses, Song of Solomon 4:16 and 5:1. Here, with equal lines of Hebrew text from the beginning of the book on one side and exactly the same number to the end on the other, we come to the heart of Solomon's Song. The focal point of the chiastic structure, these verses emphasize its major theme. Veiled in the symbolic language of "coming to the garden," they describe the happy consummation of Solomon and Shulamith's marriage.

In terms of the Song's "return to Eden" motif, the verses expand upon Genesis 2:24: "Therefore a man shall . . . be joined to his wife, and they shall become one flesh." Genesis 2 describes how God separated the man and woman from their original one flesh union. The Song of Solomon celebrates the great delight that accompanies their coming together again in all the aspects of oneness now available to them.

Invitation and response characterize these central lines. "Let my beloved come to his garden and eat its pleasant fruits" (S. of Sol. 4:16). To her invitation he responds, "I have come to my garden, my sister, my spouse" (S. of Sol. 5:1). The invitation-response pattern illuminates the nature of true love. Marriage's most intimate act uses no force, pressure, or manipulation. The physical and emotional responses of Shulamith herself offer the best evidence of the atmosphere of loving freedom that should exist in it. Into this relationship she freely and joyfully enters. "My garden" is "his garden" (S. of Sol. 4:16).

In the New Testament Paul sets forth a principle that complements the mutuality of the Song. "Let each of you look not only for his own interests, but also for the interests of others" (Phil. 2:4). In matters where we have no explicit "thus saith the Lord," this principle will guide couples in knowing how to love each other. Neither should push the other beyond that with which he or she is physically, emotionally, or spiritually comfortable. Each will seek the other's comfort, pleasure, and overall satisfaction.

The Song poetically describes the rapture of their physical communion through its most elaborate use of line parallelism:
"I have come . . .";

"I have gathered . . .";
"I have eaten . . .";
"I have drunk . . ."

The metaphors of the three ambrosia-like mixtures—myrrh and spice, honeycomb and honey, and wine and milk (S. of Sol. 5:1)—portray the absolute ecstasy of the garden experience.

In the loving commitment of one to the other in marriage, physical union elicits a response much deeper in the human heart. Elizabeth Achtemeier gives us insight into the unifying potential of the "one flesh" experience:

"In the process of sexual intercourse, we feel as if the most hidden inner depths of our beings are brought to the surface and revealed and offered to each other as the most intimate expression of our love. All we are as male or female becomes open to the other, and is made complete by being joined with the inner self of one's mate. We know each other in a way otherwise utterly impossible, and that knowing and that fulfillment carry over into our whole married life, and strengthen and deepen and periodically refresh it." [4]

Couples have often confided to us how much their intimate union has enriched their spiritual experience with God. In a sense such lovemaking can be akin to worship and praise. Ephesians 5:21 states, "Be subject to one another out of reverence for Christ" (RSV). The married love of a husband and wife especially illustrates the meaning of this text. In the act of sexual union they submit to each other in a special way, serving each other. It is a joyful celebration, a reveling in the good way God created and redeemed them as male and female. In such romance, such companionship, such committed love between husband and wife, Paul saw the key to understanding the most sublime and holy oneness ever—"This is a great mystery, but I speak concerning Christ and the church" (verse 32).

In their insightful book of devotional readings for couples, *In the Presence of God*, David and Vera Mace draw upon passages from the journal of Temple Gairdner, a missionary to Cairo during the past century. The journal reveals a deeply spiritual man who approached marriage as the Song of Songs did, with reverence and joy. As he prepared for his wedding, Gairdner prayed:

"That I may come near to her, draw me nearer to Thee than to her; that I may know her, make me to know Thee more than her; that I may love her with the perfect love of a perfectly whole heart, cause me to love Thee more than her and most of all.

"That nothing may be between me and her, be Thou between us, every moment. That we may be constantly together, draw us into separate loneliness with Thyself. And when we meet breast to breast, O God, let it be upon Thine own." [5]

---

[1] Ellen G. White, *The Adventist Home* (Nashville: Southern Pub. Assn., 1952), p. 94.

[2] Pope, *Song of Songs*, p. 117.

[3] E. J. Young, *An Introduction to the Old Testament* (Grand Rapids: William B. Eerdmans Pub. Co., 1949), p. 327.

[4] Achtemeier, *The Committed Marriage*, p. 162.

[5] Temple Gairdner, quoted in David and Vera Mace, *In the Presence of God* (Philadelphia: Westminster Press, 1985), p. 63.

CHAPTER 10

Becoming One When Two Are So Different

W e met them at a marriage retreat. He was older than she by more years than usually thought wise. And the couple, whom we will call Peter and Martha, were vastly different from each other in temperament and personality as well. While Martha was quiet in the midst of a crowd, Peter was a talker with a twinkle in his eye. He loved people and would happily have been the last to leave the church parking lot on Sabbath morning, having shaken the last hand and waved the last goodbye. Martha preferred to slip out during the closing hymn. Whether working or playing, sleeping or rising, remodeling their home or rearing their children, their ideas and habits were more often than not at odds.

Their differences had brought great difficulty into their lives together. His easygoing, spontaneous manner was at times like gravel in her shoes as they walked life's road. Unlike her husband, she was methodical, determined, decisive beneath her quiet frontage. Her headstrong way taxed the limits of his patience and aroused, more often than he liked to remember, a hot anger inside him.

Despite it all, they loved each other. But what to do about their differences? "How can we be 'one flesh' when we're so different?" they queried. Many couples have asked that same question. But lurking not far beneath it are other pressing questions not so often raised out loud. "What should we do with the conflict, the frustration, the anger, the hurt that, initially at least, the differences between us tend to spark?" And the even harder questions: What to do with the struggles within ourselves that make it so hard to accept another, to yield our own selfish desires, to find that mutuality that respects and commands respect yet keeps no score of rights or wrongs? What to do when we have hurt each other deeply, violating the spirit if not the letter of our covenant until there seems no point of return? We hear echoes of this dilemma even in the Song of Songs.

Harmony and Dissonance in the Sacred Song

Scripture upholds one all-encompassing ideal as the essence of marriage—becoming "one flesh." This tiny phrase has tremendous implications. It speaks of physical intimacy, yet much more. Emotional and spiritual bonding, mutual giving and receiving, exclusiveness, unswerving devotion, total commitment—all find themselves encompassed in this compact blueprint for marriage. Such oneness does not call for the surrender of personhood, of one becoming lost in the shadow of the other. Rather it represents a complete unity, mutuality, and harmony between two distinct persons who maintain full personhood and full equality.

Solomon's Song exalts this ideal with its major chords struck from God's majestic score composed in Paradise. Yet the Song does contain discordant notes as well, jarring dissonances that sound the failings of the earthly pair. Passages that expose personal and relational struggles lie next to verses that reflect idyllic marriage as it was meant to be, conceived in the mind of God Himself. On either side of the halcyon scenes of Solomon and Shulamith's wedding day, for example, we find episodes of stark contrast (S. of Sol. 3:1-4; 5:2-7). Her dreams reflect her concerns about the fidelity of their relationship. They vividly convey emotional pain, anger, conflict, and a terrifying sense of separation that doubtless had a basis in fact.

This mix of perfection and imperfection in the lives of the families of Scripture, this disclosure of real difficulties that get in the way of the ideal, is God's way of sharing with us the fact that in this world it will ever be so. This side of paradise, given the boundaries of our fallen state, we will always encounter a gap between the divine ideals toward which the Word of God summons us and their full realization in human experience. It is against the ever present tension between ideal and real that Solomon tuned the strings of his Song. But the salvation story tells us how, in Jesus Christ and by His grace, the two can be linked together.

Through the interplay of the ideal with the reality of one fallen couple's experience in the Song of Songs, God directs us to His grace. Grace that can present us faultless "in Christ" even as we struggle with our sinful natures, and grace that can help us grow toward the ideals of Christian marriage in an imperfect world as imperfect partners with imperfect mates. Grace that provides full assurance here and now of our ultimate salvation because "in Christ" we have been "accepted in the Beloved" (Eph. 1:6), and grace that will help us "walk in love as Christ also has loved us" (Eph. 5:2) in response to His immeasurable gift.

Becoming one flesh since Eden must always begin by acknowledging this dichotomy between heaven's ideals and our human limitations. But we don't like to do that. New lovers, both young and old, sustain the market for rose-tinted glasses. A young man swaggered into our offices, his bride-to-be in tow. "We're getting married," he announced, "but our pastor told us that before he would do our wedding, we had to come see you. What's all this stuff about premarital counseling, or whatever you call it?"

After we spent a little time getting acquainted, Ron asked both of them, "Give me several good reasons why you've decided to marry this person." The would-be groom was quick to respond. He had only one reason, he declared exultantly, and it was enough. "She's just what I've been waiting for!"

We turned to his fiancée expectantly for her reasons. She sat transfixed, a blissful, dazed look in her eyes. Eventually she reentered our planet and crooned, "I can't really think of any . . . except that he's so-o-o wonderful and we're so-o-o in love!"

To get couples beyond the "bliss barrier," to gently open their eyes so they can take a realistic look at each other—wonders and warts tied up in a single package—are important aims of both formal and informal preparation for marriage. Some are so romantically smitten it's next to impossible to get them to see reality. Others fear that a close look might spoil something. One woman remarked, "I no more want to know about Everett before marriage than I want an inventory of my Christmas presents before Christmas!"

The traditional Christian wedding vows tend to blur the distinction between the biblical ideal and reality after the Fall. They extract awesome promises from the couple: "Solemnly before God and in the presence of these witnesses do you, *full name*, take this woman (or man) to be your lawfully wedded wife (or husband), to live together after God's ordinance in the sacred estate of matrimony? Do you promise to love, comfort, honor, cherish, in sickness and in health, in prosperity or adversity, and, forsaking all others, keep yourself only for her (or him) so long as you both shall live?"

One young man's eyes widened as he contemplated such a vow just prior to his wedding and gasped, "That sounds like it was written for angels!" We certainly do not want in any way to minimize the depth of covenant Christian marriage demands. But we believe Christian family sociologist Dennis Guernsey was on to something in his commentary on wedding vows in his book *The Family Covenant*. Knowing that everyone will fail to reach such high ideals perfectly, Guernsey suggests that if wedding vows included an awareness of the frailty of all human covenants, it would spare couples much disappointment and pain.

"In some ways the wedding vows would be stated better and more realistically if they said, 'I take you to be my lawfully wedded spouse with the full knowledge that you are weak as I am weak; that you will be unfaithful as I will be, if not in actuality, then in fantasy; that there will be times when you will disappoint me gravely as I will disappoint you. But in spite of all this, I commit myself to love you, knowing your weaknesses and knowing the certainty of betrayal.'" [1]

Perhaps our compulsion to deny our inability to reach God's

ideals gets strengthened by those experiences that confirm our fears that to be anything less than perfect—at least as far as anyone else knows—will cost us acceptance and prestige in the Christian community. And perhaps, deep within us, even in the presence of our closest loved ones, we hide our flaws, frightened, as John Powell puts it, "to tell you who I am, because you might not like me and I'm all I've got."

Early in our ministry for families we spoke during prime time in the main tent at a large camp meeting. We worked hard on our presentations, wanting genuinely to help families, but also, we must admit, wanting to look good. After one of our seminars, a woman came up to talk. With a sideward glance at me, she said sincerely to Karen, "It must be really wonderful to have a husband like Ron." She went on about how special our marriage must be, how smooth-running our household, how obedient our children, how flawless my judgment and decision-making. "I wish my husband were like that," she sighed deeply, "and I wish he had been here!"

I was glad he wasn't, because I knew her compliment was ill-deserved. And I knew our presentation hadn't really helped her much. She went away with ideals reinforced perhaps, but too discouraged by the gulf that existed between the ideal and the real in her marriage to take up with courage the challenge of oneness. And I'm quite sure that if she made a report to her husband, he probably wished he could get his hands on me!

It's painful to think of how many such experiences we had to endure before we cautiously took the first steps toward self-disclosure, steps that risked criticism and rejection, misunderstanding and censure, yet steps that many have assured us may have meant the difference between despair and hope. Sharing from our personal experience has in the end become our most powerful witness to the potency of God's grace. The truth is we are all caught in our marriages between the lofty ideal of "one flesh" and the real handicaps we know as fallen human beings. Though disappointment, frustration, anger, conflict, and pain are experienced in different ways by different temperaments, none of us escapes them. But the solutions do not rest in denial. There's much better news.

A Miracle for Marriage

The good news is that what we are powerless to accomplish in ourselves can be ours in Jesus. It is He who enables Christian couples to stretch back toward Eden's one-flesh ideal. Where we are weak, He is mighty. He stands ready to work a miracle of grace in every marriage whose partners turn to Him.

Through His perfect life, death, and resurrection He has provided abundant salvation for all humankind. If you would find wholeness and restoration in your life, healing for your relationships, and oneness for your marriage, allow yourself to revel in the warm, enveloping fountain of grace cascading over our planet because God became flesh and dwelt among us, because God became sin for us, and because "in Him" we are made righteous and are reconciled to God. The balm we need in our marriages is the Balm of Gilead. It is Christ's redemptive, self-giving love, poured into our hearts by the Holy Spirit (Rom. 5:5), that is the only catalyst that can fuse two divergent hearts into one.

We cannot know unselfish love in marriage until we have dared to believe God's unconditional love for us personally. As we have come close to Christ and confronted His loveliness, the perfection of His character, the celestial ideals to which He continually calls us, the story of Peter has been a great encouragement. It can't have been easy living with Peter. Earnest, energetic, impetuous Peter, so committed—he thought—to the ideals of Christ's kingdom that he boasted of his unswerving allegiance and even took up arms in the Master's defense. Yet in Christ's time of deepest need Peter failed miserably. Gone were his undying commitment, his comfort and support, his lofty promises. But in spite of it all, Jesus loved Peter unconditionally.

"I have prayed for you" (Luke 22:32), Jesus assured Peter. Jesus knew *all* about Peter, his failures in the past, his denial in the future, the anguish just ahead for them both on that terrible Crucifixion weekend. Yet the errant disciple remained in Christ's mind as He uplifted him before God's throne.

At the echo of a cock's call, "the Lord turned and looked at Peter" (verse 61). It was a glance that convicted deeply, but also an expression of compassion and covenant love. That look sustained Peter through a long dark night of confrontation with self.

"Go and tell His disciples—and Peter—that He is going before you into Galilee" (Mark 16:7), the angel instructed Mary at the tomb on Resurrection morning. Peter's heart must have leaped with both unbelief and unbounded joy when he got the message. To have been singled out to receive the good news of the Resurrection, to still be counted among the disciples on Sunday morning after the events of Friday, was nearly incomprehensible. But that was not all. Somewhere, between the Resurrection and Christ's appearance to the 11 disciples, Jesus found Peter (Luke 24:34), and in the seclusion of a private encounter heard his confession and assured him of His love.

We too can rest in that love. Since we do not earn His love by our goodness, we can bring our burdens to Him and find respite for our souls. Refreshed at the inexhaustible fountain of His love, we may return to our marriages with new courage, new tenacity, new hope. Christ loves your marriage very much. In fact, He died to redeem it. He has a plan and purpose for our lives together, and His love frees us, motivates us, enables us to reach for the ideals of His Word. As John, the disciple whom Jesus kept on loving despite his many unlovely qualities, wrote reflectively in later life: "Beloved, if God so loved us, we ought also to love one another" (1 John 4:11).

A New View of Differences

Ultimately the way we deal with differences determines the quality of our marriages, our families, and our friendships. Differences often kindle disagreements, and disagreements can grow into anger and conflict. Anger and conflict, if unresolved, can lead to resentment, bitterness, and alienation. For some, marriage is synonymous with endless controversy and argument. For others, conflict becomes so painful that one partner capitulates to the other and surrenders his or her personality and will. Many simply withdraw from each other's lives, resigned to live parallel lives aboard ships that rarely even pass in the night. But to progress toward intimacy, we must deal with differences.

We still laugh with friends who attended an early family life workshop with us about Ron's spontaneous response to the results of some psychological testing that he and I had completed. It was one of the first times we saw our differences graphically profiled, and for Ron it was overwhelming. He held our two profiles in his hands and exclaimed, "I think this marriage may be about to self-destruct!"

Although we laugh about the fact, we are still very different! We score as almost complete opposites on every test we've taken. On one temperament inventory I score high as an "information-gatherer," while Ron is definitely a "decision-maker." It's become something of a joke between us that I travel to seminars with a briefcase loaded with books to read, hoping to glean some fresh information before we make our presentation. Ron leaves on a trip with his briefcase packed with finished notes and outlines, ready to stand up and speak. His worst fear—and it is not unfounded—is that because of some new thing I've discovered, I'll want to rewrite the notes barely minutes before we're scheduled to begin.

We would be less than honest if we didn't admit that our differences cause us times of frustration and conflict, even anger. But because we value our relationship, we are learning to look for the positives in our differences and the contributions that each can make to our relationship. Ron will admit that if we don't keep reading and studying, we're not growing. And I must confess I envy his abilities in deciding how to organize and prepare for presentation the material we've found.

Handling Anger

When we were first married, we didn't talk about anger. Likely we would have identified with one woman who responded indignantly to a seminar on anger in relationships: "Good Christians don't get angry," she declared emphatically, "and this whole discussion irritates me!" But as we have become more and more secure in each other's love, we have begun to share more deeply about its roots in our lives.

In truth, it has been our own struggle with anger that has driven us to learn all we could about how to handle it in ways that avoid damaging relationships. Karen is what experts on the subject describe as a "suppressor," one who reluctantly acknowledges anger and who tends to keep it bottled up inside until it reaches explosive proportions. I, on the other hand, am a "venter"—one who displays anger visibly in words and actions. We are learning that anger is part of our God-given emotional package, a built-in defense mechanism that guards against acceptance of abuse and a God-ordained righteous indignation in the face of injustice and impoverishment.

Like every other gift of God, sin has perverted our anger response, and Satan has often used it against us. As a passionate expression of a defensive, self-centered heart, uncontrolled by love, it ruins relationships, but rightly released and exercised, it is not a sin. Counsels Paul, "Be angry, and do not sin: do not let the sun go down on your wrath, nor give place to the devil" (Eph. 4:26-27).

In close relationships the emergence of feelings of anger ("displeasure," "irritation," "annoyance," "indignation" are synonyms) and the acknowledgment of those feelings to each other can serve an important purpose. Since anger generally stems from some sense of injustice, hurt, fear, disappointment, or frustration, it usually signals something that we should be communicating to each other. David and Vera Mace, who have been among the pioneers in helping couples learn to grow from their struggles with anger, offer this insight: "By getting behind the anger to the hurt feeling that has triggered it, the couple can learn something important about their relationship and clear it up. This is one of the most valuable ways in which relationships grow." [2]

A Balm for Hurting Relationships

Within the microcosm of marriage strife can grow to rival that between nations. Some live with physical and emotional pain, hoping that somehow things will get better. Others endure in quiet desperation, not knowing what to do. Still others divorce.

The wrenching problems that siphon happiness from so many marriages bring anguish to God's heart. Not a tear falls, not a sleepless night goes by, not a cry of despair escapes human lips, that heaven does not feel. Even in the most painful of family circumstances, in situations in which separation may even be necessary for the protection of all involved, Christ opens the way for healing and for new beginnings. He longs to spare His followers such tragedy, to find in the resources of the gospel a balm that will bring healing for the hurts we thrust into each other's lives.

The last morning devotional of the enrichment weekend Peter and Martha attended focused on forgiveness. After a period of Bible study we asked the couples first to write and then to talk together on the topic "Times in our marriage when forgiveness has meant so much" and "Areas in which forgiveness is needed in our relationship to make way for new beginnings." It was an especially moving time for Peter and Martha, and we had the privilege of prayer with them after our private times of sharing together as individual couples. God's Spirit was especially close. Martha asked for forgiveness for long-harbored hurts between her and Peter. Peter's prayer too was one of confession and a pleading with God for forgiveness and renewal in their marriage. We shall never forget the experience because their forthright prayers carried our own feelings and desires for our relationship to the throne of God as well.

In Christian marriage, partners are not perfect, but by God and by each other they may be forgiven. In Christ they can break down barriers to unity. What was true of Jew and Gentile is true of husband and wife, for "he himself is our peace, who has made the two one and has destroyed the barrier, the dividing wall of hostility" (Eph. 2:14, NIV). God, who gathers together all things in Christ (Eph. 1:10), has likewise drawn us together in Him. Marriage then becomes that setting in which a man and a woman may offer each other an experience in grace, a taste of agape love that suffers long and is kind, that bears all things, believes all things, hopes all things, and endures all things. A covenant love that never fails.

---

[1] Dennis B. Guernsey, *The Family Covenant* (Elgin, Ill.: David C. Cook Pub. Co., 1984), p. 23.

[2] David and Vera Mace, *In the Presence of God* (Philadelphia: Westminster Press, 1985), p. 58.

CHAPTER 11

A Time to Recapture Love's Delights

History credits the troubadours of twelfth- and thirteenth-century Europe with being the fathers of romance. Their dreamy, wistful ballads of the courtly love of lords and ladies quickly grew popular. The songs touched responsive chords in hearts hungering for love's passion and delight, the very qualities religious leaders believed to be incompatible with holiness. But centuries before such wandering minstrels strummed their tunes, Solomon was divinely inspired to sing his own sublime song. Listening to it, we hear of the attraction, the excitement, the tenderness, the unbounded physical and emotional joys of love. And we hear them in the context of a man and woman moving in step with the Divine design for pair-bonding. Love's deepest intimacies must remain within the covenant of marriage.

The wife's longing for the love of her husband opens and closes the Song of Solomon: "O that you would kiss me with the kisses of your mouth!" (S. of Sol. 1:2, RSV). "Make haste, my beloved, and be like a gazelle or a young stag on the mountains of spices" (S. of Sol. 8:14). Throughout the poem, both husband and wife enjoy love's sensual pleasures. Says she, "O that his left hand were under my head, and that his right hand embraced me!" (S. of Sol. 2:6, RSV). "Your head crowns you like

Carmel," declares Solomon to her, "and your flowing locks are like purple; a king is held captive in the tresses. How fair and pleasant you are, O loved one, delectable maiden!" (S. of Sol. 7:5, 6, RSV). Embedded in the heart of Sacred Scripture by God Himself, these verses declare that romantic love is biblical. Like the dazzle of a diadem that delights the eyes and lures the onlooker to the treasure reflecting the light, these qualities of romance belong to the love God made it possible for couples to enjoy—they are one with it.

The world of the troubadours is not unlike ours today. For many, the Song of Solomon's powerful depiction of romance causes uneasiness. In this arena of human love, "the devil has achieved something of a take-over bid," J. A. Motyer comments in his preface to Hudson Taylor's collection of sermons on the Song of Solomon.[1] Song, screen, and printed page—the media agents that both reflect and influence today's values—have stolen sexuality. They have stripped it of its sanctity as God's good gift to marriage and torn it from its role in helping couples bond for a lifetime. Instead they have garbed it in glitter, shaped it into the bait of commerce, and palmed it off as "love." But it is a shoddy substitute for what God intended.

It is time to recover the love of the Song of Songs, to reclaim for Christian marriage its profound joy and rapture, the utter ecstasy of love's pure delights. Emotional and physical pleasure constitute an essential part of a healthy marital bond. And they help fortify marriage against dangerous attractions lurking outside its covenantal boundaries.

The Allurement of Alien Bonds

Years ago we received a letter that tore at our hearts. It came from a family whom we had grown to love during our stay with them. In labored lines and with shaky pen, the father poured out his anguish over a tragic experience that had befallen their family. "To say it in short sentences," he wrote, "our son and his wife are in a crisis we never would have thought of. He has left the ministry. He has deeply violated his wife. He fell in love with a girl to whom he was giving Bible studies." His young wife had forgiven him, the letter went on, but the son was undecided which direction to go. "I am absolutely short of words to tell you of our feelings and our situation," the father concluded. "All is like an awful frost amid a seemingly wonderful day of spring. We are praying day and night. Write us, please. We are deeply afflicted."

Sadly, the number of families who could pen a similar letter grows daily. We did write and offered what comfort we could. And that letter caused us to commit ourselves to each other again. We wanted to do all we could to help couples avoid the disastrous consequences of infidelity and to enjoy instead an enriched experience of married love.

The Bible counsels about inappropriate relationships. Several sections of the book of Proverbs give guidance on how to avoid marital unfaithfulness and maintain a strong marriage. By this time, Solomon's heaven-bestowed wisdom had combined with the experience he had gleaned from his mistakes, and both seem to be reflected in Proverbs 5:1-14. The accounts of the adulterous affair and its consequences are so vivid that one cannot help sensing that they are likely autobiographical. Do not look for love in the wrong place, he cautions. "Drink water from your own cistern" and be "enraptured" (literally, *intoxicated*) with the love of your spouse (Prov. 5:15, 19).

Science confirms susceptibility to alien bonds. Evangelist Billy Graham, noting our age's quest for evidence to shore up faith, observed, "This generation crowds eternity and wants to know 'Why?' " Recent scientific studies of human behavior provide evidence and strengthen scriptural teaching on the topic. One thing science points out is the frailty of human bonding. Donald Joy reviews the findings:

"People who study the pair-bonding patterns of the warm-blooded Creation species command our attention. They report, among other things, that some species are so fiercely and exclusively monogamous that if a mate dies, they never re-mate, and live out a solitary existence. These are the *perfectly bonding* species and include golden eagles, marmoset monkeys, ring doves, coyotes, and wolves, among others. But biologists and anthropologists agree that while humans are distinctly monogamous, we are an *imperfectly bonding* species. That is, we are attracted to the idea of one exclusive lifelong bond, but we are vulnerable to distraction by seductive environments or relationships.'' [2]

Here we encounter both good news and bad news. The good news is that instinct alone does not govern the process of human bonding. Our close ties to one another involve the trait that makes us human—the capacity to choose. God intends that our bonds with each other should come about in the same manner as His with us—by intentional choice. We would not want it any other way. However, the bad news is that our capacities to form faithful, permanent bonds are weakened by sin. We are susceptible to alien, inappropriate bonding, possessing no natural immunity against them. Thus we need the resources of divine grace and the provisions God has made for us in order to maintain our promises to each other.

How Not to Run a Red Light

Science also confirms the personal elements involved in bonding and the way they work. We know, for example, that the development of relationships involves each of the five senses: looking at each other, hearing each other's voice, and touching each other with the hand, with an embrace, or with a kiss. Scent and taste play roles also. Other intertwined factors include the emotional warmth created by another's encouragement or affirmation that satisfies specific longings of the heart. Bonds develop out of shared life experiences: working, playing, eating, opening one's fears and hopes to each other, and even enduring hardships together.

Monitor developing relationships. Normal pair-bonding inevitably follows an instinctive pattern or script. To summarize what we learned in chapter 7: a desire to hear the other's voice follows initial eye contact. Casual touching is next, first with the hand, later with an encircling arm. The sequence continues with face-to-face contact and deeper communication. Ever-increasing trust and comfort in the other's presence leads to touching of the head and other parts of the body. The final stages involve genital intimacy.

If an inappropriate pair-bond should develop with someone

other than one's married partner, the pattern will be similar. But such predictability provides an important line of defense. One man told of the good feeling he received from calling his company supervisor. "Things hadn't been going so well at home, so I was rather down when I phoned in to the office," he said. "She detected my feelings right away. As I tried to explain how difficulties at home were affecting my sales, she told me, 'You deserve better than you're getting at home. You're really a good salesman! I'm glad you're a part of our team!' " Continuing, he related that "she comforts and encourages me. I look forward to hearing her voice." Such well-intended encouragement can, if individuals are not careful, ignite the engines of the bonding sequence.

When an extraordinary comfort, an exceptional inner delight, or an electric excitement results from seeing him or her, from hearing the other's voice, or from touching or being touched, the initial stages of bonding are under way. Charles Mylander likens the situation to that of speeding into an intersection when the traffic signal is red.[3] It's time to apply the brakes when you find yourself wanting private time with one who is "off-limits" or you find yourself sharing personal thoughts and notes or giving gifts. Daydreaming or nightdreaming of the person confirms the growing bond. Through familiarity with the physical, mental, and emotional responses of bonding and the attachment levels they signal, we can know how far we have progressed in a relationship and thus identify or stop inappropriate bonding.

Be alert to vulnerable moments. Our human weaknesses provide no excuse for sin, but an awareness of them and of situations in which we become vulnerable will aid us as Christians. Because an illicit relationship can steal up on anyone who ignores the warning signals, it should cause us to be careful in maintaining faithfulness and integrity and to seek strength from Him who "watches all [our] paths" (Prov. 5:21, RSV).

Vulnerable moments include times when one is working apart from one's spouse, when one or the other is experiencing grief or loss or in special need of affirmation, or when one or the other is sharing spiritual or emotional themes on a deep personal level.

Such circumstances are not always avoidable, but do call for special vigilance on our part.

Danger lurks near any deteriorating relationship. When the show of affection is minimal or nonexistent and the little attentions have disappeared, or when couples have stopped having fun together, the marriage is suffering. Preoccupation with petty annoyances, nagging, faultfinding, correcting each other in public, making jokes at each other's expense—all are characteristic warning signs of poor marital health. Each partner is susceptible to attention from outside the marriage bounds. Lines from a poem by Ella Wheeler Wilcox express how neglect in marriage can leave the ears of the heart open to a stranger:

> One fateful day when earth seemed very dull
> It suddenly grew bright and beautiful.
> I spoke a little, and he listened much;
> There was attention in his eyes, and such
> A note of comradeship in his low tone,
> I felt no more alone.
> There was a kindly interest in his air;
> He spoke about the way I dressed my hair.
> And praised the gown I wore.
> It seemed a thousand, thousand years and more
> Since I had been so noticed. Had mine ear
> Been used to compliments year after year,
> If I had heard you speak
> As this man spoke, I had not been so weak.[4]

The Role of Sexual Love in Marriage

Emphasizing romance in marriage will provide a good defense against sexual temptation. But the central lesson of the Song of Solomon is that such emotional and physical pleasure constitute an essential part of a healthy marital bond. While the instruction "Be fruitful and multiply" (Gen. 1:28) reminds us of the procreative purpose of human sexuality, the Song of Solomon reveals that God intended sexuality to benefit the marriage itself. The book mentions nothing of sexuality for the purpose of children. The focus is on the unitive rather than the procreative purpose of sexuality. Paul in 1 Corinthians 7:3-5, where he speaks of "conjugal rights" (RSV) and coming together again after breaking sexual relations for some specific cause such as prayer or fasting, also reflects this unitive purpose. Likewise Proverbs 5:19 affirms, "Let her affection fill you at all times with delight, be infatuated always with her love" (RSV).

Christian physician Ed Wheat and his wife, Gaye, proclaim, "You have God's permission to enjoy sex within your marriage. He invented sex; He thought it up to begin with." [5] They continue: "Although sin did enter the human race in the Garden and brought with it the possibility of perversion of every good thing (including sex), God's plan for His beloved Creation has continued to operate through the provision of the Redeemer, Jesus Christ. By faith people can choose God's way! It is true that our culture is saturated with sex distorted into lust, and desire has been twisted and deformed, until it appears as a beast running loose in the streets, destroying God-given boundaries. Nevertheless, our marriage bed is a holy place in the sight of God. We must be careful to maintain this viewpoint concerning sex in marriage, for it is God's. Hebrews 13:4 says, 'Marriage is honorable among all, and the bed undefiled. . . .' Sex in marriage is wonderfully right." [6]

Building Biblical Romance Into Marriage

Overcoming a faulty theology of sexuality is not the only hurdle couples face in building romance into their marriage. Some take marriage for granted and feel no need. Rearing children can siphon off a couple's interest in each other. Life events—furthering education, advancing a career, or building a business—may put marriage on a lower rung of priority. To nurture marriage requires an investment of energy, but after life's daily tasks a couple may not have enough energy left to give to the relationship.

One old-timer at the age of 100, when asked how long he and his wife had been married, looked with a twinkle at his companion of many seasons and replied, "Not long enough!" We like that sentiment! What can be done to keep the twinkle in the eye? How can we enhance the luster of love? Here are several ideas for building romance that we have detected in the Song of Songs.

Love so your partner feels loved. Karen greatly loves flowers and is overjoyed when I bring her some. (I used to ask why this was necessary, since she had married a "Flowers"!) My rather unromantic and practical mind devised a plan one day to save money, satisfy her wishes for a while, and still get flowers for her. I brought home an artificial arrangement. "Here," I said enthusiastically. "You can display it for as long as you like, and we will also have it for later!" Her appreciation for my rather grandiose (it seemed to me) gesture of love became evident later when I found them on a table at our yard sale. I asked why. Sensing my hurt, she shared her feelings about bargain-basement dried flowers, purple and orange in a green vase, that conflicted completely with the shades of blue decorator colors in our home. I realized then why my gift of love did not make her feel loved. It showed too little sensitivity for her tastes and feelings.

Ask yourself, "What compliment can I give, what gesture can I show, that will really make him [or her] feel loved?" Be aware of the times when he or she demonstrates appreciation. Take them as your clue. Alter your manner of showing love accordingly. The unusual compliments in the Song of Solomon obviously appealed to this couple. Solomon's compliments made Shulamith feel loved, but a wife today might not respond so enthusiastically to "your nose is like the tower of Lebanon which looks toward Damascus" (S. of Sol. 7:4)!

An important corollary, of course, is to be gracious in receiving the other's gestures of love, however short of your expectations they may fall. Karen and I have since talked over the episode with the dried flowers and have learned some valuable lessons about giving and receiving love. The way we receive a gift has a profound effect upon the giver. Blessed indeed are both when one can receive with grace another's gift though poor it may be.

Care for your personal appearance. Delight in the personal appearance of the partner plays a major role in the romance of the Song of Solomon. The couple experience and enjoy the qualities of each other over and over through the physical senses of sight, sound, scent, touch, and taste. And personal attractiveness continues to be a vital factor in marital satisfaction.

Neither should take the other's acceptance of his or her personal appearance for granted. The individual you see in the mirror is the person your wife calls her husband or your husband calls his wife. What little improvements can you make today or this week to improve your physical attractiveness?

Create a romantic setting. The setting of Solomon's and Shulamith's lovemaking exudes excitement and delight. Whether in their private chambers or amid the verdant bowers of nature, scenes of beauty, aromatic fragrances, and soothing sounds surround them. The appeal of the place enhances the romance.

During one marriage seminar we attended the leaders challenged us as couples on this point. "Go home," they said, "and take a good look at your bedroom. How appealing is it? Has it become a storeroom for household junk? How romantic is that?" They had made a good point. Our bedspread was faded and the curtains, a carryover from the last move, were not a perfect fit. Old magazines overflowed the nightstands and the walls were too bare. It was *not* very romantic. We set about to make it an inviting spot. Anticipation made even the work of redecorating fun! The importance of preparing our private place had not dawned on us before, but we look forward now more than ever to being together there.

Give the gift of time. Not long ago we asked a group of about 50 couples to list the things they'd like the most for their marriage if they could have their "druthers." The words "time together" appeared frequently. Our circumstances often tend to crowd out the time we need with each other. The question of time together evidently brought tension into the relationship of Solomon and Shulamith. The forceful imagery ("shall I be like a prostitute?") with which she makes her appeal indicates the couple's urgent need for time together and her intuitive sense that without it their relationship will die (S. of Sol. 1:7). The issue surfaces again in the frightful dream (S. of Sol. 5:2-7). Now he wants time with her, but she makes herself unavailable.

Happily married couples determine to carve out little niches of time to be alone. What is needed is nonproblem, nonpressure time, when your hearts can tune up together, when you can just listen to each other's feelings. It can be sitting together on the sofa after dinner, walking, canoeing, watching a sunset, looking at old picture albums, or dining out. Attending one of the growing number of marriage enrichment events will ensure a number of hours for learning, growing, and sharing.

A friend of ours gets our award for the most romantic mini-vacation. On one occasion, without his wife knowing it, he arranged for the care of their children, packed their suitcases (including several of her favorite outfits), and drove to a quaint hotel he had discovered in a nearby town. Renting one of the nicest suites, he adorned it with some scented candles and a beautiful bouquet of flowers. That evening he invited his wife to go on an after-dinner business appointment with him, promising to stop at one of her favorite shopping places.

Routing himself past the inn, he said, "Isn't that an unusual hotel! Wouldn't it be great to stay there sometime?"

"It sure would," she responded enthusiastically.

"Hey, let's see what it's like inside!" he suggested, pulling the car up to its front entrance. The friendly innkeeper invited them to inspect a room and . . . You can guess the rest! Their eyes still sparkle as they relate their story of that romantic surprise.

Gift-giving is important to romance, but no gift is as meaningful as the gift of yourself to your partner. Find times and places for sharing what is on your hearts. Laugh together. Recover love's excitement and delight from whatever would rob you of romance. Let that special one in your life hear often, "You are precious to me. Out of all the others I have chosen you, and I would do so again!"

[1] J. A. Motyer, in J. Hudson Taylor, *Union and Communion* (London: China Inland Mission, 1891), p. v.

[2] Donald Joy, *Unfinished Business* (Wheaton, Ill: Victor Books, 1989), p. 150.

[3] Charles Mylander, *Running the Red Lights* (Ventura, Calif.: Regal Books, 1986), p. 35.

[4] Ella Wheeler Wilcox, "An Unfaithful Wife to Her Husband," in Mylander, p. 31.

[5] Ed Wheat, M.D., and Gaye Wheat, *Intended for Pleasure* (Old Tappan, N.J.: Fleming H. Revell, 1977), p. 20.

[6] *Ibid.*, p. 23.

CHAPTER 12

More Than Birds and Bees

O n the only occasion in which Shulamith's brothers speak in the Song of Songs, they describe her as a child:

We have a little sister,
And she has no breasts.
What shall we do for our sister
In the day when she is spoken for?

If she is a wall,
We will build upon her
A battlement of silver;
And if she is a door,
We will enclose her
With boards of cedar (S. of Sol. 8:8, 9).

We do not know if it is because of cultural custom that her brothers sense a responsibility for her developing sexuality, or perhaps it may be because they have assumed responsibility in place of the father who appears to be absent from the household. This much seems clear, however: They want the best for her both in her childhood and as she grows into womanhood. Intuitively they sense it means a responsibility to prepare and educate her as she develops sexually.

Preparing a Child's Bonding Surface

We have come to think of such nurture and guidance for sexuality as readying a child's "bonding surface" for future relationships. It is primarily and ideally the privilege of parents. Like a carpenter who spreads the cement evenly and allows it to dry unmolested until the right moment for joining two surfaces he wants to glue, so parents may carefully prepare their child for good bonding experiences in the years ahead.

Birth bonding. The process begins at birth when, within a matter of minutes after entrance into the world, a child discovers the warmth of his or her mother's embrace. Fortunate is the child who enjoys during the first two or three almost magical hours all manner of hugging and kissing, cooing and caressing, snuggling and mutual admiring, in the arms of both mother and father.

God wrote the script for the human bonding experience and planted it in the hearts of both parents and babies. In most instances, mothers, fathers, and newborns need only to be together, and they will intuitively know what to do. Soon relationships with siblings will round out the family circle. From its earliest moments, life is preparing the bonding surface that will enable a child to have a lifetime of fulfilling relationships.

Early positive messages. Our friend Alberta Mazat, a marriage and family therapist who has specialized in the area of sexuality, offers wise and sensitive counsel to parents in her books *That Friday in Eden* and *Questions You've Asked About Sexuality*. We have borrowed the title for this chapter from her and credit her inspiration and expertise for many of the ideas that follow. Also we highly recommend her books to families seeking Christian answers to questions about sexuality and about better ways of approaching the subject within the family circle. Regarding the important preparatory work begun as parents send their children early positive messages about their bodies, Mazat makes the following suggestion:

"Parents have a wonderful opportunity early in their care of their babies to include a good feeling about their bodies. By patting, stroking, and caressing, they demonstrate not only their loving concern, but the realization that their little ones can experience good body feelings. Meeting needs in a consistent, tender way teaches trust. Using loving tones and smiling chatter demonstrates the joys of communication. Each of these early experiences . . . can be part of the preparation for good sexuality later in life." [1]

Unfolding the Good News

As children grow, parents may gradually unfold the good news about sexuality. It is good to be a girl, and it is good to be a boy, we must communicate to them. While girls and boys have differences in their bodies, both are special. As Mr. Rogers explains to children who watch his television program: "Girls are fancy on the inside, boys are fancy on the outside. Everybody's fancy. Everybody's fine." Our distinctly sexual body parts and functions have proper names. We don't need to be embarrassed or shy about them, though there are appropriate and inappropriate times and places to talk about and uncover them.

Before children go to school, Alberta Mazat suggests we add to their growing knowledge the facts that "babies grow inside their mothers, but are a product of both Mommy and Daddy" and that "mommies can nourish their babies through breast-feeding." [2]

Young children must also realize that they should not allow anybody to touch their genital area. Give them permission to say an emphatic no to any such attempt and instruct them to run and tell another adult about it no matter what the offender may say.

Middle childhood's crucial years. The years of middle childhood, after children start school, open many opportunities for teaching about the wonder of the human body and for developing within boys and girls a sense of responsibility for the care of their bodies. In an era when parents had little instruction on how to teach their children about sexuality, Ellen White highly recommended to parents an article from the *Health Reformer* of January 1873. It decried the ignorance of young girls about their development and expressed chagrin at the subtle messages conveyed to children by their parents' unwillingness to share information about sexuality.

The author noted the zeal with which Christians endeavored to show God's handiwork in nature, but—speaking of young

girls—said, "of themselves, 'God's noblest work,' they are left
in ignorance. Better far, that as little children, they should be
taught of their own structure and development . . . and taught to
trace it in God's loving mind and hand, than at the age when they
most need care and sympathy, when mysterious feelings are
pressing upon them, and the great questions of life arise before
them, that they should be forced to learn from playmates those
things which it should be a mother's privilege to teach, and of the
sacredness of which they cannot have too high a conception!" [3]

Middle childhood is a period of rapid intellectual development and intense curiosity, a good time for learning firsthand
how animals are born, and of the tender loving care human babies
need to grow and develop. Further expansion of the story of the
development of a baby should include information about the role
of the father and of internal fertilization.

This is an important time for the establishment of same-sex
friendships. They give assurance that it is good to be a boy or girl
during a period when boys and girls tend to spurn each other's
company. We found a wonderful folder of "documents" in our
attic that dated to this period in our sons' development. Ron had
built them a tree house in the side yard that was the envy of every
boy in the neighborhood. Soon a boys' club headquartered in the
branches, and its members whiled away the hours creating secret
codes and maps and schemes for keeping out girls. There was one
notable exception, however. They allowed one girl membership,
mostly because her brother often couldn't come over without her.
But we discovered when we unearthed the records that the boys
had obliged her to sign an official declaration that—on penalty of
immediate expulsion—she would *never* act like a girl!

Sexuality in Adolescence: Living, Learning, Making Choices

However, as surely as the tree in which their tree house
nestled will sprout leaves in the spring, this stage will come to an
end. One day, in what may seem the twinkling of an eye,
members of the opposite sex who were once so intolerable
suddenly turn beautiful and handsome and really quite nice. So to
same-sex friends young people will now add opposite-sex friends

who affirm developing manhood and womanhood in other important ways.

Prior to the onset of puberty children need to know about the changes it will bring. Parents will want to prepare the way for the commencement of menstruation for girls and seminal emissions in boys. They should explain such changes as a natural part of growing up female and male, ways in which nature readies the body for its adult sexual role. Those parents who talk openly with their children about the physical and emotional changes adolescence will produce, prior to its beginning, will open the way for their children to come to them with their questions and concerns as the physical changes do occur. Acceptance and affirmation by parents, particularly that of the opposite sex parent or parent figure, are never more important than during this awkward stage when most young people are convinced that the entire world is watching them.

Early adolescence is a period for rounding out a fuller understanding of the male and female reproductive system and the basic principles of birth control. It is a time for a growing understanding of personal worth that leads to an enlarging respect both for oneself and for others. Boy-girl relationships will expand, ideally in group activities that allow for many friendships to develop and many opportunities for social interaction. Late in adolescence, education regarding sexuality moves further into the realm of understanding what it means to be in love, learning about deepening levels of intimacy and trust, and making responsible decisions regarding sexuality.

A wall or a door? During adolescence when youth confront intensifying drives and many choices, parents the world over can identify with Shulamith's brothers. Their concerns are the same as that of those brothers in antiquity: Will my child be a wall or a door? Will my child guard his or her chastity, pace his or her march toward maturity with appropriate levels of intimacy, proceed step by step according to God's design? Or will my child be a door, offering easy, premature access to physical intimacies apart from the maturity, commitments, and responsibilities of the marriage covenant? How can I help my child to see that choices made today affect both his or her future and that of his or her friends?

But parents are not alone in their concerns. We have discovered that youth the world over have related questions of their own, though they may not openly share them. What is God's plan for my sexuality? How can I know for sure that His plan is the best? That it is right for me? How can I please God, my parents, my friends, and do what I want to do all at the same time?

Shulamith reached an important conclusion that left no doubt about her values. In no uncertain terms she resolutely declares, "I am a wall" (S. of Sol. 8:10). She speaks for the countless young men and women who have resisted the attractions and the pressures around them and reserved love's deepest intimacies for marriage. On their wedding night Solomon confirms her own declaration in words that express the joy to be known by those who wait:

A garden enclosed
Is my sister, my spouse,
A spring shut up,
A fountain sealed (S. of Sol. 4:12).

Her decision to guard her chastity until the day she is mature enough to give herself to her chosen husband in a covenant relationship of love "as strong as death" (S. of Sol. 8:6) is apparently not, in the end, one forced upon her by her brothers' determination to fortify or contain her. Rather, it is her own choice, based upon her personal understanding and acceptance of the divine laws governing the emotional and physical makeup of human beings. Note that she pauses three times throughout the Song, in the intensity of the most intimate lovemaking described in the poem, to offer an appeal to those who walk the path toward marital intimacy behind her: "Do not stir up nor awaken love until it pleases" (S. of Sol. 2:7; 3:5; 8:4).

It is as though the experience of intimacy itself corroborates what she has believed all along. Physical oneness involves the giving of one's total being to another, a giving too complete and too risky apart from lifelong covenant. Here again, the observations made by students of the human bonding process and from personal experience lend credence to Shulamith's beliefs and the wisdom of God's design that places the "one flesh" experience only within the context of the marriage covenant.

More than a decade ago, after our children started school, I worked on the staff of *Insight* magazine. Ron and I have reflected many times on one manuscript that made a lasting impression on me. I do not know the name of the young author, though I corresponded with her at the time and have often thought of her. I want you to hear her story in her own words.

"When I started going with Jason, I didn't have any problem saying no to him. . . . But as we became very close, it got terribly hard for me to stop at my set limit. After a while I just didn't. . . . Anyway, I was sure that he was the one for me.

"The first time we 'went all the way' was great for the moment. . . . When it was over, Jason looked at me and said, 'Now we have to get married.' . . . We prayed earnestly for forgiveness and a clean, new chance. But damage had been done. The next time emotions ran high we either couldn't stop or didn't want to. . . . We had given everything, and since we were too young to get married, our relationship turned stale. . . .

"I gave myself to Jason because I loved him. . . . I've tried to convince myself that Jason destroyed me. But I know a relationship works both ways. . . . Now I'm worried about a lot of things beyond the pain of the moment, such as what will happen if I ever fall in love again. Will I be able to trust another person, risk being hurt? How will I ever tell him about my past? Can I live intimately without telling? . . .

"I never thought that I would be talking this way—I, the happy-go-lucky rebel. I feel kind of desperate inside that you won't hear what I really have to say. About how awful it is to feel robbed of the mystery of the future, of your dignity, worth, and self-respect. I loved Jason and gave so much. Healing is going to take a long time. It just isn't worth the tears.

"I'm only 15 years old." [4]

One does not have to listen to the stories of too many teenagers caught in the web of premarital sexual activity to recognize that in most instances pain is the ultimate consequence. Donald Joy notes that the journey through deepening levels of

friendship and trust toward marital intimacy is like taking a trip
on a toll road or in a taxi. The further you travel, the higher the
fare. When relationships break off, as they most often do during
the teen years, the degree of hurt and pain experienced by the
couple is in proportion to the level of intimacy they have known.
Donald Joy marks the stage at which couples begin to dream
together about the future as the last point a couple can depart from
the intimacy highway before the toll exacted in emotional pain
increases sharply.[5]

When intimacies run too deep too early, there is a great risk
that the bond formed may be weak and vulnerable.[6] Marriage
counselors confirm that many couples who have engaged in
premarital sex have lingering undercurrents of mistrust and
whirlpools of anxiety that can haunt a marriage for years. For the
promiscuous, the risks are also high. As individuals repeatedly
wrench apart bonds tightly fused by sexual intimacy, they may do
such damage to the bonding surfaces of those involved that it may
affect their future capacities to bond permanently. Only the
healing touch of grace can overcome such damage.[7]

A few years ago an academy invited me to share in presenting
a seminar to academy students on dating and sexuality. The
school assigned me the opening presentation, and as I stood
before the large assembly of teens, I experienced one of those
moments of deepening insight into the love of God. God, our
young people need to be assured, is 100 percent for love! 100
percent for sexuality! It was with great joy that He bestowed this
gift on the human family in the beginning, and it is with great
delight that He continues to impart its energies and blessings
again and again as every new baby is formed male or female in
the mother's womb, as every child develops into manhood or
womanhood, as every couple leave father and mother and
become one flesh. It is a gift born of His very essence—agape
love. But it is a keepsake designed to unfold across a lifetime like
the petals of a rose. Only as growing maturity, responsibility, and
measures of commitment time-release the full fragrance of
deepening levels of intimacy will its aromas sweeten life's
journey.

God's Forgiveness and Grace: The Second Message

This good news is our first message, and we must get it to our young people while they still have time to make right choices, before they have had to experience the hard consequences that often accompany deep levels of intimacy apart from the protection of the marriage covenant. Our other, equally important task is to bring a second message of hope to those whose choices have already brought pain and confusion into their lives.

I cherish in my files a letter signed "one encouraged teenager" from the young author of the *Insight* article. Her story so touched our staff that we had to reply. Thankful that she had provided a return address, we drafted a letter to her. It read in part:

"You expressed your feelings and worries so clearly as you wrote, we hurt with you. Mostly we hope you could know God feels with you too, and that He loves and accepts you even though you have been through this experience. While there are tears, even scars, the wonderful thing about our God is that He can heal and restore, even help you forgive yourself as He has forgiven you, and open the way for fulfilling relationships for you in the future. Thank you for sharing yourself; we hope you can feel our love—and God's—even across the miles."

Alberta Mazat extends the possibility of "spiritual revirgination" to youth who have recognized that their paths have strayed from God's plan.[8] The radical forgiveness of a God who casts sins into the "depths of the sea" (Micah 7:19) always provides for new beginnings, no matter what the mistake. Teens await our encouragement that this message can really be true for them. The letter from "one encouraged teenager" is only one piece of evidence that they greatly need and eagerly receive the "second message."

When it came time to close that opening presentation to the academy convocation, my eyes focused, as they had many times, on a row of young men and women seated at the front. Undoubtedly they had been assigned their seats. Yet they had graciously given me their attention, and now I searched for words to send them away with something to think about. I believe that what I shared is a pretty good bottom line.

"Next time you're with someone you really care about and find yourself wanting more, remember that wanting more is not wrong. You were created for more. But the more that you seek can be found only in completing the developmental cycles of love built into you by your Creator, who will never deny you any good thing. It was Jesus who came so that we might have life and have it more abundantly. You must ask yourself, 'What is the more I'm really after?' "

---

[1] Alberta Mazat, *Qestions You've Asked About Sexuality* (Boise, Idaho: Pacific Press Pub. Assn., 1991), p. 9.

[2] *Ibid.*, p. 13.

[3] In Mazat, *That Friday in Eden*, p. 139.

[4] *Insight*, Feb. 5, 1980.

[5] *Bonding: Relationships in the Image of God*, p. 47.

[6] _____, *Unfinished Business*, p. 98.

[7] *Ibid.*, pp. 153-157.

[8] Mazat, *Questions You've Asked About Sexuality*, p. 51.

CHAPTER 13

Love Aflame

In what may be the Song of Solomon's climactic movement, Shulamith poignantly cries out,

> Set me as a seal upon your heart,
> As a seal upon your arm;
> For love is as strong as death, . . .
> Its flames are flames of fire,
> A most vehement flame (S. of Sol. 8:6).

Her figure of love as a "vehement flame" presents a vivid image for everyone who has ever witnessed a roaring blaze. Fire fighters who have confronted a raging inferno know firsthand how relentless and unstoppable is its rampage through tall timber in a dry season. Love, says the Song of Solomon, is like that, but in a good sense. It is mighty and powerful, fiercely unyielding, invincible. Vanquishing all that stands in its way, its flame cannot be extinguished. Earthly fortunes cannot approach its true value.

> Many waters cannot quench love,
> Nor can the floods drown it.
> If a man would give for love
> All the wealth of his house,
> It would be utterly despised (verse 7).

127

Love That Transcends Human Limitations

The passage is a sublime crescendo in the Song's poetic lines, but something is lost in the translation. A friend for whom English is a second tongue lamented one day the impoverishment of our language when it comes to the word "love." She shook her head sadly as she told us how incomprehensible it would be in her language to use the same word for "I love you" between lovers and "I love ice cream" among connoisseurs! Scripture is much more precise in its concepts of love, drawing clear distinctions between human love and love born from above.

The love that Shulamith longs for takes in the human sentiment and pleasurable emotions familiar in the Song of Songs, but it also aspires to the loftier dimensions of strength, permanence, and boundlessness that transcend emotion and arise from the will. Both the Old and New Testaments associate these qualities with God's agape love, but while they are natural to God, they seem quite out of the reach of fallen human beings. "I have loved you with an everlasting love," the Lord assures His people (Jer. 31:3). "God is love," declares the apostle John of the divine nature (1 John 4:8, 16). But of fallen human beings Jesus verifies, "I know you, that you do not have the love of God in you" (John 5:42). However, as He did Peter, so the Saviour has included us in His prayers. "I have declared to them Your name," He apprises the Father, "and will declare it, that the love with which You loved Me may be in them, and I in them" (John 17:26).

Human love is conditional. Sin binds and limits human love. The only love of which we are humanly capable is a *conditional* love, a love with a string attached. We dish it out and receive it in proportions carefully measured to match what we feel is earned or deserved.

Karen and I are latecomers to the computer age. Intimidated at first, we now seem helpless apart from one. So ingenious are such machines that at times they act almost alive. I find myself expecting my computer to anticipate my needs, and when it doesn't, I have words with it! Each computer has what experts call *default values*, baseline parameters that its makers have pro-grammed in it. Unless specifically commanded to do otherwise, a computer follows its programming—it *defaults* to its internally predetermined settings. The computer I'm using, for instance, produces wider page margins than I like. I keep telling myself that someday I'm going to take the time to find out how to change the default settings. As it is now, I have to adjust margins each time I begin a new document. In a sense, human beings are like that when it comes to loving. We default to conditional love. Douglas Cooper describes the limitations of such love:

"Without God, human love, no matter how professedly pure, no matter how deep the degree of emotion that accompanies it, always has a qualification, an 'if,' a price tag attached. This destroys its potential to meet anything but the surface needs of others. It cannot heal. It cannot uplift. It cannot save. It is limited to loving only the 'lovable' and only as long as they remain 'lovable.' Its inadequacy eventually leaves men to perish without hope." [1]

God's love is unconditional. The greatest of all good news is that no conditions limit God's love—it is *unconditional*. God loves human beings just as they are—selfish, hostile, hateful, rebellious, unkind, critical, disobedient, disbelieving. The cross of Christ contrasts in bold relief the conditional love of human beings with God's unconditional love: "Very rarely will anyone die for a righteous man, though for a good man someone might possibly dare to die. But God demonstrates his own love for us in this: While we were still sinners, Christ died for us" (Rom. 5:7, 8, NIV). Listen for the compassion in the tones of God's words through the prophet Hosea, and do not miss the implied contrast between a human response to unfaithfulness and that of God: "How can I give you up, Ephraim? How can I hand you over, Israel? . . . My sympathy is stirred. I will not execute the fierceness of My anger. . . . For I am God, and not man, the Holy One in your midst" (Hosea 11:8, 9). The story of Hosea and Gomer is about God's love. But it is also about how God's love can become our own. "Love her," God instructed Hosea as he grieved over his wayward wife Gomer, "as I, the Lord, love the Israelites although they resort to other gods" (Hosea 3:1, NEB). What an invincible, unquenchable flame of love!

Called to Love Unconditionally

The human bent toward conditional love poses the greatest challenge to our ability to accept the gospel. One cartoon in a religious periodical pictured a Pharisee boasting, "We get our righteousness the old-fashioned way—we *earn* it!" Although we smile, at the same time we sense that somehow the cartoon has laid bare the natural condition of our hearts. Fear may mask our conditional inclination—fear that God has only made provision for our salvation, and that our security really lies in our ability to have enough faith, to surrender completely enough, to trust God fully enough, to study, pray, give, witness, or change enough to find acceptance with Him. But the good news we can know today is that God gives us the freedom to choose to accept or reject His grace, when faith extends a hand to accept that grace, it receives a free gift, made available solely on the merits of Jesus Christ.

"Our dependence is not in what man can do; it is in what God can do for man through Christ. . . . We are not to be anxious about what Christ and God think of us, but about what God thinks of Christ, our Substitute. Ye are accepted in the Beloved." [2]

Jesus told a story in Matthew 18:23-35 about a great debtor who received an incredible gift presented in the spirit of unconditional love. Imagine the dizzying experience of being released from a debt that had hung about your neck like a millstone for as long as you could remember. A debt that had haunted your dreams and absorbed every activity of your life. As the story unfolds, the debtor, not unlike us, cannot seemingly grasp the magnitude of the gift. So, the Bible records, he leaves the presence of the gracious king in the same mind-set in which he had entered. *I must repay* is all he can think, and he seeks to exact from a fellow debtor a pittance owed to him. The lesson lay in the sad words of the beneficent king: "Should you not also have had compassion on your fellow servant, just as I had pity on you?" (Matt. 18:33). The call of the gospel is for us to accept the unconditional love of God toward us, and to pass it on. God calls Christians to be great lovers!

Becoming a Lover for God

They were not unlike family, that band of 12 Jesus called

friends. Like most families, they had their good times. But they also struggled with quarrels and bitterness, reservations and hatred. Some were bigoted, deceitful, disloyal. Others succumbed to manipulation and chauvinism, pride and selfishness. Discouragers dampened enthusiasm, and the stubborn stirred up tension. Ultimately, betrayal and abandonment marked their response to the Saviour's deepest moment of need. But "Jesus," Scripture says, "having loved His own, . . . He loved them to the end" (John 13:1).

This depth of commitment, this level of tenacity, this unquenchable love of which Shulamith speaks and which is demonstrated in its fullness in the life of Jesus Christ, shines like a planet in the heavens, elevating our eyes, setting our sights on the perfect ideal toward which we must stretch. But God has not left us alone.

Before His death Jesus promised a Comforter who would abide with us forever (John 14:16). "He will testify of Me. . . . He will glorify Me, for He will take of what is Mine and declare it to you" (John 15:26-16:14), Jesus continued. And a fruit or demonstration of His presence among us will be love (Gal. 5:22).

It is as the heart opens to the love of Jesus that transformation occurs. Zooming in on one face in the midst of Jesus' disciple family, we follow the profile of the apostle John. Thanks to paintings like Da Vinci's *The Last Supper,* I suppose, we persist in thinking of him as the lovable sort, but John was anything but that! "Evil temper, revenge, the spirit of criticism, were all in the beloved disciple. He was proud, ambitious to be first in the kingdom of God. But day by day, in contrast with his own violent spirit, he beheld the tenderness and forbearance of Jesus." [3]

Four times John refers to himself as if in wonder as the disciple Jesus kept on loving (John 13:23; 19:26; 20:2; 21:7). Again and again Jesus responded to John's need for unconditional love and reached out to touch his heart. The Saviour drew him into the inner circle of the disciples, showed him His glory on the Mount of Transfiguration, and summoned him in the Garden of Gethsemane to witness the most vulnerable moment of His life on earth. As He hung on the cross, He gave His own

mother into John's care. Jesus demonstrated to him unbounded
acceptance, trust, confidence, and love.

But it was the cross that changed John's heart forever. There
Jesus became sin for John, became his Saviour. There He took his
untamed spirit, his hasty temper, his prejudice, his thirst for
power and revenge. On that cross hung, as it were, the Son of
Thunder (Mark 3:17), that at the foot of the cross, cleansed in the
stream of redemptive, transforming love that flowed from Jesus'
pierced side, John might become by grace a son of God. It was
in the shadow of the cross, that John and this motley band went
forth to turn the world upside down in the name of this Lover of
our Souls.

Too often our families are constrained by all that bound the
twelve. Few of us are far removed from the tragedies of
parent-child estrangement, separation and divorce, violence and
abuse, the helplessness of seeing relationships crumble yet not
knowing where to turn for help. Many feel they have loved nearly
to the point of laying down their lives, and still it hasn't seemed
to make any difference. Meanwhile, too often we unwittingly
intensify the hurts in our quickness to judge and our concern more
for who's to blame than how to be about a ministry of healing.
Ours is a profoundly imperfect and fallen world. There will
always be families who cannot endure. Our responsibility is to
reach out a hand in love to bind up broken hearts, to strengthen,
to encourage, and to comfort. To walk side by side the path
toward healing.

But there will also always be the call of the ideal. Through us
all God wants to show His love to the world. Countless people
around us long for a vision of His love. They search for models
of what it means to be a Christian family. They hunger for human
affection and embrace. Jesus' question penetrates the centuries:
"You are the world's seasoning, to make it tolerable. If you lose
your flavor, what will happen to the world?" (Matt. 5:13, LB).

The house next to ours has had a number of occupants in the
13 years we have lived here. We were especially sad when a
family we had come to love moved across town, but looked
forward with anticipation to meeting our new neighbors. Seeing
the man of the house walking into the yard, Ron walked up and

extended his hand to introduce himself. "Hi, I'm Ron Flowers, welcome to our . . ." but he was cut short in mid-sentence and left with his hand awkwardly proffered. The man said nothing, simply lengthened the lead on the leashes of his two Dobermans and walked straight ahead.

Though a bit baffled, Ron recovered, but this first encounter marked the tenor of our relationship with this man as long as we knew him. We did visit betimes over the back fence with his wife who seemed to want our friendship, but it is their little boy who lingers in my memory. Years separated his age from that of either of our boys, so from the beginning they considered him a bit of a pest. He was always waiting in the backyard when they returned from school, eager to see if they would play basketball with him or perhaps—even if reluctantly—invite him in for a few minutes. I do believe he would have moved in with us if he could.

One day, rounding the corner from the kitchen into the living room, I was startled to find the little boy simply sitting on the couch by himself. He had obviously let himself in the front door without a sound. "Why, Darron, I didn't know you were here!" I exclaimed as my pulse returned to normal.

"Oh, please Mrs. Flowers, let me stay," he pleaded with his words and his eyes. "I like to sit in here because it's pretty and nobody's fighting." I drew him close to me and assured him he could stay as long as he liked. At the same time I grieved over the times I had been quick to send him packing because he was in the way of my agenda.

Darron and his family simply vanished from our neighborhood one day. No one knows where they have gone. The house has new owners again, and it would be easy to just forget. But somehow I keep hoping that because Darron witnessed at our house a man and a woman who love each other, two boys who laughed and played and knew they could take their parents' love for granted, that because he has seen it once, it could be true for him in the home he will one day establish. Even if it wasn't happening at his house, being near it should count for something.

We may have just uncovered one of God's big reasons for placing a love story in the heart of the Old Testament. In the love

of Solomon and Shulamith for each other, there is occasion for all
of us to be near true love at least once, that we may dare to
believe happiness can exist between two people even if we have
never witnessed it on earth. And having understood, to see the
curtain drawn back on the agape love of God.

Not far from Ron's boyhood home in New Brunswick the
highest tides in the world rise and fall in Fundy National Park.
The grandeur is awesome when they peak, the mud flats dismal
as they ebb. Human love is like the tide. In the seasons when love
crests we are sure nothing could ever wrench us apart, but in the
seasons when love ebbs, we may wonder if anything can hold us
together.

At Fundy National Park the tides rushing up the Petticodiac
get all the press. We seldom reflect on the reality that tides, as
impressive as they may be, are a phenomenon of the edges. The
great ocean from which they surge is deep and wide, constant in
its mighty presence, unmoved by turmoil at its outer rim.

It is from the great unchangeable ocean of God's love that we
may draw when the tide ebbs in our relationships. His love
"suffers long and is kind; . . . does not envy; . . . does not parade
itself, is not puffed up; does not behave rudely, does not seek its
own, is not provoked, thinks no evil; does not rejoice in iniquity,
but rejoices in the truth; bears all things, believes all things, hopes
all things, endures all things. [His] love never fails" (1 Cor.
13:4-8). It is a love to set the universe singing! In Him, it can be
our own.

---

[1] Douglas Cooper, *Living God's Love* (Mountain View, Calif.: Pacific Press Pub. Assn.,
1975), pp. 38, 39.
[2] Ellen G. White, *Selected Messages* (Washington, D.C.: Review and Herald Pub. Assn.,
1958), book 2, pp. 32, 33.
[3] _____ , *The Desire of Ages* (Mountain View, Calif.: Pacific Press Pub. Assn., 1940),
p. 295.

APPENDIX

Dialogue in the Song of Songs

Authorship:
1:1 The song of songs, which *is* Solomon's.

Shulamith:
1:2 Let him kiss me with the kisses of his mouth—
For your love *is* better than wine.
1:3 Because of the fragrance of your good ointments,
Your name *is* ointment poured forth;
Therefore the virgins love you.
1:4a Lead me away!

Daughters of Jerusalem:
1:4b We will run after you.

Shulamith:
1:4c The King has brought me into his chambers.

Daughters of Jerusalem:
1:4d We will be glad and rejoice in you.
We will remember your love more than wine.

Shulamith:
1:4f Rightly do they love you.
1:5 I *am* dark, but lovely,
O daughters of Jerusalem,
Like the tents of Kedar,
Like the curtains of Solomon.

1:6 Do not look upon me, because I *am* dark,
Because the sun has tanned me.
My mother's sons were angry with me;
They made me the keeper of the vineyards,
But my own vineyard I have not kept.
1:7 Tell me, O you whom I love,
Where you feed *your flock*,
Where you make *it* rest at noon.
For why should I be as one who veils herself
By the flocks of your companions?

Daughters of Jerusalem:
1:8 If you do not know, O fairest among women,
Follow in the footsteps of the flock,
And feed your little goats
Beside the shepherds' tents.

Solomon:
1:9 I have compared you, my love,
To my filly among Pharaoh's chariots.
1:10 Your cheeks are lovely with ornaments,
Your neck with chains *of gold*.
1:11 We will make you ornaments *of gold*
With studs of silver.

Shulamith:

1:12 While the king *is* at his table,
My spikenard sends forth its
fragrance.

1:13 A bundle of myrrh *is* my beloved to me,
That lies all night between my
breasts.

1:14 My beloved *is* to me a cluster
of henna *blooms*
In the vineyards of En Gedi.

Solomon:

1:15 Behold, you *are* fair, my
love!
Behold, you *are* fair!
You *have dove's* eyes.

Shulamith:

1:16 Behold, you *are* handsome,
my beloved!
Yes, pleasant!
Also our bed is green.

Solomon:

1:17 The beams of our houses *are*
cedar,
And our rafters of fir.

Shulamith:

2:1 I *am* the rose of Sharon,
And the lily of the valleys.

Solomon:

2:2 Like a lily among thorns,
So is my love among the
daughters.

Shulamith:

2:3 Like an apple tree among the
trees of the woods,
So *is* my beloved among the
sons.
I sat down in his shade with
great delight,
And his fruit *was* sweet to my
taste.

2:4 He brought me to the banquet-
ing house,
And his banner over me *was*
love.

2:5 Sustain me with cakes of rai-
sins,
Refresh me with apples,
For I *am* lovesick.

2:6 His left hand *is* under my
head,
And his right hand embraces
me.

2:7 I charge you,
O daughters of Jerusalem,
By the gazelles or by the does
of the field,
Do not stir up nor awaken
love
Until it pleases.

2:8 The voice of my beloved!
Behold, he comes
Leaping upon the mountains,
Skipping upon the hills.

2:9 My beloved is like a gazelle
or a young stag.
Behold, he stands behind our
wall;
He is looking through the
windows,
Gazing through the lattice.

2:10 My beloved spoke, and said
to me:
Rise up, my love, my fair
one,
And come away.

2:11 For lo, the winter is past,
The rain is over *and* gone.

2:12 The flowers appear on the
earth;
The time of singing has come,
And the voice of the turtle-
dove
Is heard in our land.

2:13 The fig tree puts forth her
green figs,
And the vines *with* the tender
grapes
Give a good smell.
Rise up, my love, my fair
one,
And come away!

2:14 "O my dove, in the clefts of
the rock,
In the secret *places* of the
cliff,
Let me see your countenance,
Let me hear your voice;
For your voice *is* sweet,
And your countenance *is*
lovely."

2:15 Catch us the foxes,
The little foxes that spoil the
vines,
For our vines *have* tender
grapes.

2:16 My beloved *is* mine, and I *am*
his.
He feeds *his flock* among the
lilies.

2:17 Until the day breaks
And the shadows flee away,
Turn, my beloved,
And be like a gazelle
Or a young stag
Upon the mountains of Be-
ther.

3:1 By night on my bed I sought
the one I love;
I sought him, but I did not
find him.

3:2 "I will rise now," *I said*,
"And go about the city;
In the streets and in the
squares
I will seek the one I love."
I sought him, but I did not
find him.

3:3 The watchmen who go about
the city found me,
To whom I said,
"Have you seen the one I
love?"

3:4 Scarcely had I passed by
them,
When I found the one I love.
I held him and would not let
him go,
Until I had brought him to the
house of my mother,
And into the chamber of her
who conceived me.

3:5 I charge you,
O daughter of Jerusalem,
By the gazelles or by the does
of the field,
Do not stir up nor awaken
love
Until it pleases.

Friends:

3:6 Who *is* this coming out of the
wilderness
Like pillars of smoke,
Perfumed with myrrh and
frankincense,
With all the merchant's fragrant powders?

3:7 Behold, it *is* Solomon's
couch,
With sixty valiant men around
it,
Of the valiant of Israel.

3:8 They all hold swords,
Being expert in war.
Every man *has* his sword on
his thigh
Because of fear in the night.

3:9 Of the wood of Lebanon
Solomon the King
Made himself a palanquin:

3:10 He made its pillars *of* silver,
Its support *of* gold,
Its seat *of* purple,
Its interior paved *with* love
By the daughters of Jerusa-
lem.

3:11 Go forth, O daughters of
Zion,
And see King Solomon with
the crown
With which his mother
crowned him
On the day of his espousals,
The day of the gladness of his
heart.

Solomon:

4:1 Behold, you *are* fair, my
love!
Behold, you *are* fair!

137

You *have* dove's eyes behind your veil.
Your hair *is* like a flock of goats,
Going down from Mount Gilead.

4:2 Your teeth *are* like a flock of shorn *sheep*
Which have come up from the washing,
Every one of which bears twins,
And none *is* barren among them.

4:3 Your lips *are* like a strand of scarlet,
And your mouth is lovely.
Your temples behind your veil
Are like a piece of pomegranate.

4:4 Your neck *is* like the tower of David,
Built for an armory,
On which hang a thousand bucklers,
All shields of mighty men.

4:5 Your two breasts *are* like two fawns,
Twins of a gazelle,
Which feed among the lilies.

4:6 Until the day breaks
And the shadows flee away,
I will go my way to the mountain of myrrh
And to the hill of frankincense.

4:7 You *are* all fair, my love,
And *there is* no spot in you.

4:8 Come with me from Lebanon, *my* spouse,
With me from Lebanon.
Look from the top of Amana,
From the top of Senir and Hermon,
From the lions' dens,
From the mountains of the leopards.

4:9 You have ravished my heart,
My sister, *my* spouse;
You have ravished my heart
With one *look* of your eyes,
With one link of your necklace.

4:10 How fair is your love,
My sister, *my* spouse!
How much better than wine is your love,
And the scent of your perfumes
Than all spices!

4:11 Your lips, O *my* spouse,
Drip as the honeycomb;
Honey and milk *are* under your tongue;
And the fragrance of your garments
Is like the fragrance of Lebanon.

4:12 A garden enclosed
Is my sister, *my* spouse,
A spring shut up,
A fountain sealed.

4:13 Your plants *are* an orchard of pomegranates
With pleasant fruits,
Fragrant henna with spikenard,

4:14 Spikenard and saffron,
Calamus and cinnamon,
With all trees of frankincense,
Myrrh and aloes,
With all the chief spices—

4:15 A fountain of gardens,
A well of living waters,
And streams from Lebanon.

Shulamith:

4:16 Awake, O north *wind*,
And come, O south!
Blow upon my garden,
That its spices may flow out.
Let my beloved come to his garden
And eat its pleasant fruits.

Solomon:

5:1a I have come to my garden, my sister, *my* spouse;
I have gathered my myrrh with my spice;

I have eaten my honeycomb
with my honey;
I have drunk my wine with
my milk.

Daughters of Jerusalem:
5:1b Eat, O friends!
Drink, yes, drink deeply,
O beloved ones!

Shulamith:
5:2 I sleep, but my heart is
awake;
It is the voice of my beloved!
He knocks, *saying,*
"Open for me, my sister, my
love,
My dove, my perfect one;
For my head is covered with
dew,
My locks with the drops of
the night."
5:3 I have taken off my robe;
How can I put it on *again*?
I have washed my feet;
How can I defile them?
5:4 My beloved put his hand
By the latch *of the door*,
And my heart yearned for
him.
5:5 I arose to open for my be-
loved,
And my hands dripped *with*
myrrh,
My fingers with liquid myrrh,
On the handles of the lock.
5:6 I opened for my beloved,
But my beloved had turned
away *and* was gone,
My heart went out *to him*
when he spoke.
I sought him, but I could not
find him;
I called him, but he gave me
no answer.
5:7 The watchmen who went
about the city found me.
They struck me, they
wounded me;
The keepers of the walls

Took my veil away from me.
5:8 I charge you,
O daughters of Jerusalem,
If you find my beloved,
That you tell him I *am*
lovesick!
Daughters of Jerusalem:
5:9 What *is* your beloved
More than *another* beloved,
O fairest among women?
What *is* your beloved
More than *another* beloved,
That you so charge us?

Shulamith:
5:10 My beloved *is* white and
ruddy,
Chief among ten thousand.
5:11 His head *is like* the finest
gold;
His locks *are* wavy,
And black as a raven.
5:12 His eyes *are* like doves
By the rivers of waters,
Washed with milk,
And fitly set.
5:13 His cheeks *are* like a bed of
spices,
Like banks of scented herbs
His lips *are* lilies,
Dripping liquid myrrh.
5:14 His hands *are* rods of gold
Set with beryl.
His body is carved ivory
Inlaid *with* sapphires.
5:15 His legs *are* pillars of marble
Set on bases of fine gold.
His countenance *is* like Leba-
non,
Excellent as the cedars.
5:16 His mouth *is* most sweet,
Yes, he *is* altogether lovely.
This *is* my beloved,
And this *is* my friend,
O daughters of Jerusalem!

Daughters of Jerusalem:
6:1 Where has your beloved gone,
O fairest among women?

Where has your beloved
   turned aside,
That we may seek him with
   you?

Shulamith:
6:2 My beloved has gone to his
     garden,
     To the beds of spices,
     To feed *his flock* in the gar-
      dens,
     And to gather lilies.
6:3 I *am* my beloved's,
     And my beloved *is* mine.
     He feeds *his* flock among the
      lilies.

Solomon:
6:4 O my love, you *are* as beauti-
     ful as Tirzah,
     Lovely as Jerusalem,
     Awesome as *an army* with
      banners!
6:5 Turn your eyes away from
     me,
     For they have overcome me.
     Your hair *is* like a flock of
     goats
     Going down from Gilead.
6:6 Your teeth *are* like a flock of
     sheep
     Which have come up from the
     washing;
     Every one bears twins,
     And none *is* barren among
     them.
6:7 Like a piece of pomegranate
     Are your temples behind your
     veil.
6:8 There are sixty queens
     And eighty concubines,
     And virgins without number.
6:9 My dove, my perfect one,
     Is the only one,
     The only one of her mother,
     The favorite of the one who
     bore her.
     The daughters saw her
     And called her blessed,

The queens and the concu-
   bines,
And they praised her.
6:10 Who is she *who* looks forth as
     the morning,
     Fair as the moon,
     Clear as the sun,
     Awesome as *an army* with
     banners?

Shulamith:
6:11 I went down to the garden of
     nuts
     To see the verdure of the val-
     ley,
     To see whether the vine had
     budded
     And the pomegranates had
     bloomed.
6:12 Before I was even aware,
     My soul had made me
     As the chariots of my noble
     people.

Friends:
6:13a Return, return, O Shulamite;
     Return, return, that we may
     look upon you!

Shulamith:
6:13b What would you see in the
     Shulamite
     As it were, the dance of the
     double camp?

Solomon:
7:1 How beautiful are your feet in
     sandals,
     O prince's daughter!
     The curves of your thighs *are*
     like jewels,
     The work of the hands of a
     skillful workman.
7:2 Your navel *is* a rounded gob-
     let
     Which lacks no blended bever-
     age.
     Your waist *is* a heap of wheat
     Set about with lilies.

7:3   Your two breasts *are* like two
fawns,
Twins of a gazelle.

7:4   Your neck *is* like an ivory
tower,
Your eyes *like* the pools in
Heshbon
By the gate of Bath Rabbim.
Your nose *is* like the tower of
Lebanon
Which looks toward Damas-
cus.

7:5   Your head *crowns* you like
Mount Carmel,
And the hair of your head *is*
like purple;
The king *is* held captive by *its*
tresses.

7:6   How fair and how pleasant
you are,
O love, with your delights!

7:7   This stature of yours is like a
palm tree,
And your breasts *like* its clusters.

7:8   I said, "I will go up to the
palm tree,
I will take hold of its
branches."
Let now your breasts be like
clusters of the vine,
The fragrance of your breath
like apples,

7:9a   And the roof of your mouth
like the best wine.

Shulamith:

7:9b   The wine goes *down* smoothly
for my beloved,
Moving gently the lips of
sleepers.

7:10   I *am* my beloved's,
And his desire *is* toward me.

7:11   Come, my beloved,
Let us go forth to the field;
Let us lodge in the villages.

7:12   Let us get up early to the
vineyards;
Let us see *if* the vine has bud-
ded,

Whether the grape blossoms
are open,
And the pomegranates are in
bloom.
There I will give you my
love.

7:13   The mandrakes give off a fragrance,
And at our gates *are* pleasant
fruits,
All manner, new and old,
Which I have laid up for you,
my beloved.

8:1   Oh, that you *were* like my
brother,
Who nursed at my mother's
breasts!
If I should find you outside,
I would kiss you;
I would not be despised.

8:2   I would lead you *and* bring
you
Into the house of my mother,
She *who* used to instruct me.
I would cause you to drink of
spiced wine,
Of the juice of my pomegran-
ate.

8:3   His left hand *is* under my
head,
And his right hand embraces
me.

8:4   I charge you,
O daughters of Jerusalem,
Do not stir up nor awaken
love
Until it pleases.

Friends:

8:5a   Who *is* this coming up from
the wilderness,
Leaning upon her beloved?

Solomon:

8:5b   I awakened you under the apple tree.
There your mother brought
you forth;
There she *who* bore you
brought *you* forth.

Shulamith:
8:6   Set me as a seal upon your
          heart,
          As a seal upon your arm;
          For love *is as* strong as death,
          Jealousy *as* cruel as the grave;
          Its flames *are* flames of fire,
          A most vehement flame.
8:7   Many waters cannot quench
          love,
          Nor can the floods drown it.
          If a man would give for love
          All the wealth of his house,
          It would be utterly despised.

Shulamith's brothers:
8:8   We have a little sister,
          And she has no breasts.
          What shall we do for our sis-
          ter
          In the day when she is spoken
          for?
8:9   If she *is* a wall,
          We will build upon her
          A battlement of silver;
          And if she *is* a door,
          We will enclose her
          With boards of cedar.

Shulamith:
8:10   I *am* a wall,
          And my breasts like towers;
          Then I became in his eyes
          As one who found peace.
8:11   Solomon had a vineyard at
          Baal Hamon;
          He leased the vineyard to
          keepers;
          Everyone was to bring for its
          fruit
          A thousand *pieces* of silver.
8:12   My own vineyard *is* before
          me.
          You, O Solomon, *may have* a
          thousand,
          And those who keep its fruit
          two hundred.

Solomon:
8:13   You who dwell in the gar-
          dens,
          The companions listen for
          your voice—
          Let me hear it!

Shulamith:
8:14   Make haste, my beloved,
          And be like a gazelle
          Or a young stag
          On the mountains of spices.

Basic text from New King James Version.